MYRA STREET

THE COMPLETE RICE COOKBOOK

MYRA STREET

THE COMPLETE RICE COOKBOOK

NEW BURLINGTON BOOKS

A QUINTET BOOK

Published by New Burlington Books
6 Blundell Street, London N7

ISBN 0 906286 73 5

Reprint 1989

This book was designed and produced by
Quintet Publishing Limited
6 Blundell Street, London N7

Art Director Peter Bridgewater
Editor Nicholas Law
Photographer John Heseltine
Illustrator Lorraine Harrison

Typeset in Great Britain by
Central Southern Typesetters, Eastbourne
Colour origination in Hong Kong by
Universal Colour Scanning Limited, Hong Kong
Printed in Hong Kong by Leefung-Asco
Printers Limited

Contents

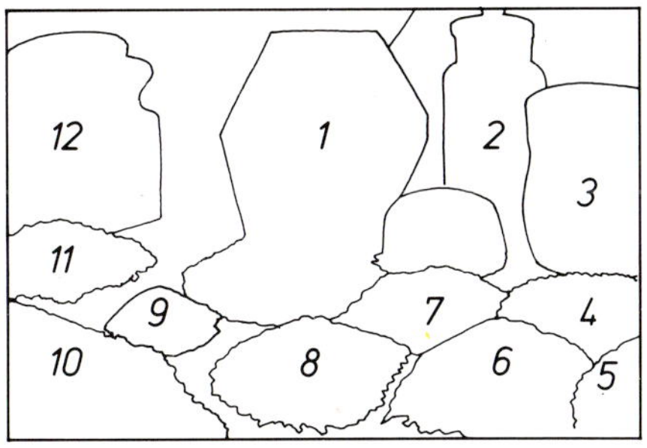

Key to pages 6-7
1 Long-grain and wild rice, mixed
2 Brown rice
3 Risotto rice
4 and 5 Pre-fluffed long-grain rice
6 Long-grain rice
7 Basmati rice
8 Parboiled long-grain rice
9 Ground rice
10 Parboiled American brown rice
11 Milled 'Patna' long-grain rice
12 Short-grain 'Carolina' rice

Introduction

RICE

RICE

Rice is one of the oldest foods known to man and forms the staple diet for well over half the human race. It is therefore undeniably the world's most important food. There are around 40,000 different varieties of rice grains and it is not surprisingly one of the most versatile of the cereal crops.

Rice was cultivated in China as far back as 5,000 BC and may originally have been found wild in the foothills of the Himalayas. It took many centuries and the development of trade routes from the Far East to bring rice to Europe, where it first emerged as a popular and widely known food around the 17th century. Now internationally popular, rice features in the cooking of Spain, Italy, Portugal and South America as well as the oriental countries.

Rice is an essential buffer food with many Chinese, Indian and oriental dishes. As a lover of delicately spiced food, I have included many recipes that are variations of dishes oriental in origin, with short cuts when possible. Many oriental dishes take a long time to prepare because of the importance of marinating ingredients. It is usually easy to organize the necessary preparatory stages in advance and the results certainly justify any extra effort.

As it requires no preparation and is so easily stored in the home, rice is the ideal food for busy cooks. There is no wastage — any leftover rice quickly becomes the base for a rice/vegetable dish, a rice salad, or with additions, a savoury meal. Many people cook double quantities for just this reason.

Rice is easy to digest and the processed form which does not require washing, if cooked with the minimum liquid, retains most of the nutrients. For those who are still more health conscious, brown rice (see page 11) is the most nutritious of all.

Mastering the art of cooking rice well is a must for the serious cook, and yet few students, experienced and inexperienced alike, are entirely relaxed about cooking this simple food. Timing is crucial with rice cookery. It is advisable to follow instructions carefully for the first few times that you cook rice and to watch it carefully while it is cooking.

One of my favourite party dishes is a version of the Indonesian Ricetafel. This can be made up with several spicy dishes such as saté, a mild curry, some sambals and a fried or boiled rice dish. Vegetable dishes can be added in all sorts of combinations to suit all tastes.

Rice has at last lost its image of a super-starchy food and can be sensibly included in calorie controlled diets. ¼ cup/50g/2oz of rice can replace 25g/1oz bread or 20g/¾oz crispbread in a day's calorie controlled diet. ⅛ cup/25g/1oz cooked (boiled) rice contains 35kcal/150kJ and approximately 8.4 units carbohydrate.

Rice is so good to eat — it is a source of quick energy, it contains some protein and the important B vitamins — and as the perfect foil for so many fish, meat and vegetable dishes, it really deserves to be part of your weekly menu.

RICE, RICE, RICE

Rice is one of the easiest foods to cook, and yet many people find themselves with a glutinous mess at the end of the cooking time. This may have something to do with the many varieties available and the confusion arising over the specially processed types which are now on sale. It is advisable to read the packet when buying rice to ensure that you have selected the correct grain for your purpose.

MAIN TYPES OF RICE
long-grain (Patna) rice
long-grain brown rice
basmati rice (all long-grain rice)
Italian risotto rice
'Carolina' or short-grain rice (both short-grain rice)
ground rice
rice flour
rice flakes
wild rice

RICE

LONG-GRAIN RICE

This is a white long-grain rice which has been milled to remove the husk, the germ and most of the layers of bran. This process is known as polishing and the grains emerge long and thin with an opaque appearance.

It is still sometimes referred to as Patna rice after the district in north-east India where it originated, but is now more often simply called long-grain rice as rice has not been exported from that part of India for many years. Most long-grain rice comes from the USA and Thailand; it is also grown in China, Australia, Guyana, India, Pakistan and Burma.

Long-grain rice should be fluffy and light after cooking and the grains should remain separate. It is used to accompany suitable savoury dishes such as stews, casseroles, curries and vegetables and it is also a good addition to salads. Many savoury composite dishes are made up with fish, meat and vegetables with rice as the main ingredient, eg paella.

BOILED RICE

Absorption method

Ingredients
1 cup/250g/8oz long-grain rice
¼–1 tsp salt
2½ cups/600ml/1pt water

To prepare

♦ Wash the rice well in a sieve or colander under the cold tap and drain.

♦ Bring the water to the boil with the salt.

♦ Add the rice to the boiling water and stir through with a fork until the water comes to the boil again. Allow it to boil for about 1 minute. Reduce the heat to allow the rice to simmer very gently for at least 12 minutes. Most of the water should be absorbed after this time; test a grain for tenderness. If the rice is still undercooked, sprinkle 2 tablespoons boiling water on to it and allow to simmer for a further 2 minutes. Keep the rice covered and leave it to stand for 10 minutes. Fork through gently. The grains should be fluffy and separate.

Water method
1 cup/250g/8oz long-grain rice
10 cups/21/4pt water
½–1 tsp salt

♦ Wash the rice and drain it as described in the previous cooking method.

♦ Sprinkle the rice into the boiling salted water and fork through until it comes back to the boil. Stir through with a fork from time to time, while cooking it for about 12 minutes. Test the grains to see if they are cooked sufficiently. Pour the rice into a large sieve or colander and rinse with fresh boiling water. The rice can then be placed in an ovenproof dish which has been oiled or buttered, covered with greased foil or greaseproof paper and placed in a moderate oven 180°C/350°F/Gas 4 for 20 minutes.
NB This is also a useful way to re-heat rice for a dinner party.

If you are willing to buy slightly more expensive rice, there are many types of processed rice which are guaranteed to cook perfectly by the absorption method. These are called pre-fluffed, par-boiled, easy cook and non-stick to name a few. They have all been treated to a steam-type pressure cooking which stops the grains sticking together.

They may however still take longer to cook than ordinary rice.

If using this type of rice it is important to read the instructions on the packet and cook accordingly.

BAKED RICE

This is a much slower method of cooking rice but it can be useful and fuel-saving when you are cooking other dishes in the oven at the same time.

Ingredients
1 cup/250g/8oz long-grain rice
½ tsp salt
2½ cups/600ml/1pt boiling water
oven temperature 180°C/350°F/Gas 4

To prepare

♦ Sprinkle the rice into an overproof casserole and then pour on the salted boiling water. Stir round with a fork.

♦ Cover well with a lid. If the lid does not fit tightly enough, place a layer of foil over the casserole or dish and then replace the lid.

♦ Cook the pre-washed long-grain rice for 25-30 minutes or until the grains are fluffy and separate.

♦ A knob of butter may be added and the rice grains tossed with a fork just before serving.

RICE

BOILED RICE (PRE-WASHED AND PRE-FLUFFED VARIETIES

On many tests of these varieties, I have found that for 1 cup of rice you will need 2 cups of boiling water and ½ teaspoon salt or ½ cup/100g/4oz long-grain rice to 1¼ cups/300ml/½pt water and ½ teaspoon salt. The cooking time by the absorption method is usually 15 minutes. Sprinkle the rice into the boiling salted water and stir round with a fork, cover with a lid and allow to cook on a low simmering heat for 12–15 minutes without stirring or removing the lid. If all the liquid has not been absorbed during that time, continue cooking for a further 2–3 minutes. Fork through until the rice is separate and fluffy.

STEAMED RICE

Ingredients

1 cup/250g/8oz long-grain rice

2½ cups/600ml/1pt boiling water

½ tsp salt

To prepare

♦ Sprinkle the rice into the saucepan with the boiling salted water, bring back to the boil and allow it to simmer covered on a low heat for 5 minutes. Drain.

♦ Bring water to the boil in a large saucepan which will take a steamer or colander. If you are using a colander with larger holes, line it with foil which has had small holes pierced in it or a new rinsed J-cloth.

♦ Place the rice in the steamer above the boiling water. Make holes in the rice with the handle of a wooden spoon to allow the steam to circulate. Cover and allow to cook over simmering water for 40–50 minutes. Turn into a warmed serving dish and fluff with a fork.

Steamed rice accompanies Chinese dishes well. Steaming is an inappropriate method for cooking large quantities as the steam will not penetrate the rice sufficiently.

Boiled rice

LONG-GRAIN BROWN RICE

This is the long-grain rice which has been milled solely to remove the inedible husk. It used only to be sold in health food shops but is now more widely available in supermarkets. This less-refined variety of rice retains some roughage, valuable B vitamins, minerals and a small amount of protein.

Brown rice has a distinctly nutty flavour. It is less fluffy when cooked than other rices and it has a slightly chewy texture in the mouth. It looks very similar to any other long-grain rice but is a soft brown colour. Do not be alarmed if there is a slightly odd smell while cooking.

There are now several varieties of the easy-cook type available and these usually have specific cooking instructions on the packet.

BOILED LONG-GRAIN BROWN RICE

Ingredients
1 cup/250g/8oz long-grain brown rice
2½ cups/600ml/1pt water
½ tsp salt

♦ Wash the rice well under the cold tap (unless it is pre-washed) and drain.

♦ Bring the water to the boil and sprinkle in the rice and the salt. Fork through to separate the grains, bring the water back to the boil for about a minute, cover the pan and turn the heat to very low. Allow it to simmer for about 40 minutes and then test a few grains. All the water should have been absorbed; however, if the rice is not cooked, add 2 tablespoons boiling water and continue cooking for a further 3–5 minutes.

Note Brown rice usually takes longer than white to cook, but there are now quick-cook varieties on the market which require only about 15 minutes.

Brown rice is excellent in salads and can always be substituted for white rice.

BASMATI RICE

This is the name given to a long-grain rice which is grown in Pakistan and India. It has a distinctive taste and is excellent with oriental spicy dishes — as pilau rice or biriani. It is often said to be the prince of rices.

Basmati rice grains are slimmer than ordinary long-grain rice and the colour is a definite white. The grains are particularly light and fluffy when cooked and basmati rice can be used in any recipe calling for long-grain rice. It is slightly more expensive but the extra taste and texture are worth it.

BOILED RICE

Cook as for long-grain rice by the absorption method, but only for 10 minutes. If using the oven method, basmati rice will take about 25 minutes.

ITALIAN RISOTTO RICE

This is a short-grain rice ideal for recipes in which liquids have to be absorbed eg risotto dishes using any well-flavoured stock. It is not necessary to wash this rice before use.

Risottos are cooked on top of the stove as the liquid has to be added gradually as the rice thickens — they have to be stirred and watched throughout the cooking time. Risottos commonly take their name from the town or area in Italy where they originated.

GROUND RICE

Ground rice is made by a prolongation of the milling process until the white rice becomes a little more granular than flour.

Ground rice is used for milk puddings and with flour for baked dishes.

MILK PUDDING

Ingredients
2½ cups/600ml/1pt milk
¼ cup/50g/2oz ground rice
1 tbsp/25g/1oz sugar
¼ tsp cinnamon
2 tbsp/25g/1oz butter
oven temperature 180°C/350°F/Gas 4

To prepare

♦ Heat the milk in a saucepan without boiling.

♦ Butter an ovenproof dish which may have fruit or jam in the bottom or not, as liked.

♦ Sprinkle the ground rice into the milk and continue stirring until the mixture comes to the boil and thickens. Remove from the heat.

♦ Stir in the sugar and turn into the ovenproof dish, sprinkle with cinnamon and dot with butter. Bake for 25 minutes.

CAROLINA OR SHORT-GRAIN RICE

Short-grain pudding rice has a round plump grain of chalky appearance. The name 'Carolina' was given to pudding rice as it originally came from Carolina. This rice has not been imported from there to the UK since the last war and a lot of it is now grown in China and Australia.

The cooked grains are moist and tend to stick together and are therefore perfect for sweet dishes, desserts, sweet or savoury rissoles and croquettes.

BASIC RICE PUDDING

Ingredients

¼ cup/50g/2oz short-grain rice

1 tbsp/25g/1oz sugar

2½ cups/600ml/1 pt milk

¼ tsp nutmeg

2 tbsp/25g/1oz butter

oven temperature 150°C/300°F/Gas 2

To prepare

♦ Grease an ovenproof dish, sprinkle in the rice and sugar, stir in the milk and if possible allow to stand for 1–3 hours in the refrigerator to help promote a creamy texture.

♦ Sprinkle on the nutmeg and dot with butter.

♦ Cook for 30 minutes and then remove from the oven and stir. Return and bake for a further 1½ hours.

Serves 4

RICE FLOUR

This is a fine flour milled from white rice which can be used in baked goods such as cakes and buns. It is sometimes used in rice cream puddings.

RICE FLAKES

This is a form of flaked rice and is not widely used in Western-type cooking. It can be used in spicy dishes with pulses and functions generally as a thickening agent.

WILD RICE

This is not a true rice as the seeds come from a wild aquatic plant. It is an expensive food and is often served with game and poultry. It requires long, slow cooking. The appearance is that of a long greyish green seed.

COOKING WILD RICE

Ingredients

1 cup/250g/8oz wild rice

1 tsp salt

3¾ cups/900ml/1½pt water

To prepare

♦ Wash the wild rice several times in a sieve and allow it to drain. Again, read packet instructions as some brands are already pre-washed.

♦ Boil the salt and water together in a saucepan, sprinkle the rice slowly into the water and bring it back to the boil. Cover and simmer over a low heat for about 40 minutes until tender.

Serves 4

Note There is now a product on sale which is a mixture of long-grain and wild rice. It makes a most interesting accompaniment for any savoury dish and is excellent in salads.

CATERING QUANTITIES

Long-grain rice, white, brown and basmati, swells to about three times its original size when cooked. This means that ⅛ cup/25g/1oz raw rice will become 6 tbsp/75g/3oz when cooked.

Allow an average of ¼ cup/50g/2oz raw rice per person if it is a side dish or just a little less in mixed rice dishes with more than 450g/1lb mixed vegetables, meat or fish.

Measures

If you prefer to measure your rice in cups, use the same measuring implement for the water as for the rice ie cook 1 cup raw rice in 2 cups water.

Allow ⅛ cup/25g/1oz per person for salads and savoury rices up to 12 people. For each additional person cook another 1 tbsp/15g/½oz raw rice.

For rice salads as part of a buffet, 3 cups/650g/1½lb will be sufficient for 25 portions.

Short-Grain Rice

Use ¼ cup/50g/2oz raw rice to 2½ cups/600ml/1pt milk for 4 portions or 6 tbsp/75g/3oz raw rice to 3¾ cups/900ml/1½pt milk for 6 portions.

COOKING HINTS FOR RICE

♦ Do read the packets and if you have easy-cook or parboiled rice follow the instructions given by the manufacturer.

♦ Wash only non-processed rice.

♦ If you are going to boil rice, use the correct amount of water or liquid and make sure it is boiling.

♦ Cover the rice tightly with a lid and do not remove until the cooking time is almost up.

♦ Stir the rice only when it goes into the saucepan but not during the cooking or it will tend to become mushy.

♦ Do not leave the cooked rice in the cooking saucepan for longer than 10 minutes after it has cooked unless you want a large cake of grains stuck together. Do fork into a heated serving dish.

♦ Use a fork to fluff rice and not a spoon. A wooden fork is very good — I have an old salad fork specially for this purpose.

The easy-cook pre-fluffed varieties are slightly more expensive but it is worth gaining confidence by trying these first. Always test the rice before the advised cooking time.

No kitchen cupboard is complete without several packets of rice. Quick meals can be conjured up in the event of the arrival of unexpected guests. Rice keeps well for long periods of time provided that it is kept dry. After a little experimentation with rice, you will be surprised at the amazing variety of dishes which can be added to everyday menus.

COOKING RICE IN THE MICROWAVE OVEN

Use the absorption method ie 2 measures of boiling water to 1 measure of rice. Cover with pierced cling film (plastic wrap), or a glass lid if using a microwave dish. Most long-grain rice takes 20–25 minutes, Basmati rice takes about 5 minutes less. The results are perfect every time and the rice can be served directly from the microwave to the table.

It is advisable to check timings in your own microwave instruction book.

YELLOW RICE

Saffron is traditionally used to flavour and colour rice but it is now so expensive that it has been widely replaced by yellow food colouring. For spicy savoury dishes turmeric may be added to give a good colour but this also flavours the rice slightly. Add the colouring to the boiling water and you will soon discover the right quantity for the shade of yellow required. Start by trying ¼–½ teaspoon turmeric *or* 6 drops yellow vegetable food colouring to each 2½ cups/600ml/1 pint water.

Ritzy Basics

Pilaf

HERBED RICE

Ingredients
1–1¼ cups/225–275g/8–10oz long-grain rice
1 tsp salt
4 tbsp/50g/2oz butter
1 onion, peeled and finely chopped
1 clove garlic, crushed
8 spring onions (scallions), washed
4 tbsp freshly chopped parsley
8 basil leaves, chopped

To prepare

♦ Cook the rice in 4½ cups/1l/1¾pt boiling water, with 1 good teaspoon salt added. Leave the pan uncovered and fork the rice occasionally for first 10 minutes.

♦ Heat the butter in a frying pan and cook the onion and garlic over a low heat for 3 minutes. Add the finely chopped spring onions.

♦ Mix the onion mixture and the rice well. There should still be a little water left.

♦ Cover with a lid and allow the remaining water to be absorbed. This will take another 5–7 minutes over a low heat.

♦ Remove the lid and taste to make sure rice is tender. Add the parsley and basil leaves. Season with freshly ground black pepper and extra salt if necessary.

Serves 4

Herbed rice may be served with grilled poultry or meat. Vegetarians may consider mixing the rice directly with some grated cheese instead.

PILAF

Ingredients

4 tbsp/50g/2oz butter

1 medium onion, peeled and thinly sliced

1 cup/225g/8oz long-grain rice

salt and freshly ground pepper

a pinch of saffron or a few drops of yellow food colouring

2 cups/450ml/¾pt stock

oven temperature 180°C/350°F/Gas 4

To prepare

♦ Use an ovenproof casserole for cooking this dish. Heat 3 tbsp/40g/1½oz butter and cook the onion over a low heat for 4 minutes. Add the rice and continue stirring for another 3 minutes.

♦ Season well. Add the saffron or colouring to the stock. Then pour the stock on to the rice and mix well with a fork. Bring to the boil. Cover and cook in the oven for about 15 minutes until stock is absorbed and rice grains are separate.

To serve

Add the remaining butter and, if you wish, 1 tablespoon grated cheese.

Serves 4

Variation

Another version of this savoury rice can be made by adding mushrooms, peppers or grated carrot to the onion. Alternatively add small strips of meat or ham to the rice or even flaked fish or prawns.

Herbed rice

RISOTTO

Ingredients
1 tbsp olive oil
2 tbsp/25g/1oz butter
1 medium onion, peeled and finely chopped
1½ cups/350g/12oz Italian risotto rice
3¾ cups/900ml/1½pt chicken stock
salt and freshly ground pepper
1 tbsp freshly chopped parsley (optional)

To prepare

♦ Using a heavy-bottomed saucepan, heat the oil and butter. Add the onion and cook over a low heat for about 3–4 minutes without browning.

♦ Add the risotto rice dry and stir fry for about 2 minutes over a medium heat.

♦ Add half the hot chicken stock. Stir from the bottom to avoid sticking and continue to do so until the grains are separate and the stock is absorbed.

♦ Continue adding the remaining stock with 1 teaspoon salt bit by bit, stirring all the time, until it is all absorbed. The risotto should have cooked to a creamy consistency in about 25 minutes without becoming mushy.

To serve

Add the freshly ground pepper and, if you wish, a little freshly chopped parsley for colour.

Serves 4

Variation

RISOTTO MILANESE

To prepare

Cook as above but substitute ⅔ cup/150ml/¼pt white wine for the equivalent stock. Add 2 tbsp/25g/1oz butter and 3 tbsp/25g/1oz parmesan cheese at the end of the cooking time just before serving. Serve with Osso Buco (see page 86). Can be garnished with mushrooms.

Osso buco
Risotto Milanese with mushrooms

PILAU RICE

Ingredients

1 cup/225g/8oz long-grain rice
2 tbsp vegetable oil
1 onion, peeled and finely chopped
1 clove garlic, crushed
½ tsp cumin
¼ tsp turmeric
½ fresh chili pepper, crushed or finely chopped (optional)
¼ tsp ground coriander
1 tsp salt
2½ cups/600ml/1 pint stock or boiling water

To prepare

♦ Wash the rice and allow it to soak for 20–30 minutes. Drain in a sieve, shaking from time to time.

♦ Heat the oil in a pan on a medium heat and fry the onions and garlic until golden brown.

♦ Add the drained rice, turn the heat down and stir in well. Add the cumin, turmeric, chili pepper and coriander.

♦ Mix the salt with the boiling liquid and gradually add to the rice. Bring to the boil and simmer, covered, over a low heat for 15–20 minutes, until the rice is cooked. Fluff with a fork.

Serves 4

Variation

Vegetable Pilau can be made by adding peas, beans, carrots, peppers, potatoes or a combination of any favourite vegetables. It is advisable to cut the potatoes and carrots into small dice, and blanch them for 4 minutes to ensure that they become cooked through. Add the chopped vegetables to the onion and garlic, and cook all together in 6 tablespoons oil over a low heat before adding the rice.

A further ½ teaspoon salt should be added to the stock, and ½ teaspoon garam masala and 2 tablespoons chopped coriander will add extra flavour.

FRIED RICE

This is an ideal way to make a delicious savoury rice dish with left-overs.

Ingredients
3 tbsp vegetable oil
1 large onion, peeled and finely chopped
1 cup/225g/8oz cooked long-grain rice
salt and freshly ground pepper
1 tbsp soya sauce
⅓ cup/50g/2oz chopped, cooked ham
⅓ cup/25g/1oz bamboo shoots
⅓ cup/50g/2oz cooked shrimps

To prepare

♦ Heat the oil in a large frying pan. Cook the onion over a medium heat until it is a pale golden colour.

♦ Add the long-grain rice and stir in with the onion. Season well.

♦ Stir in the soya sauce, ham, bamboo shoots and shrimps. Cook until golden brown. Taste for flavour. Add more soya sauce, vegetables, meat or fish if necessary.

Serves 4

Fried rice

Ritzy Vegetables

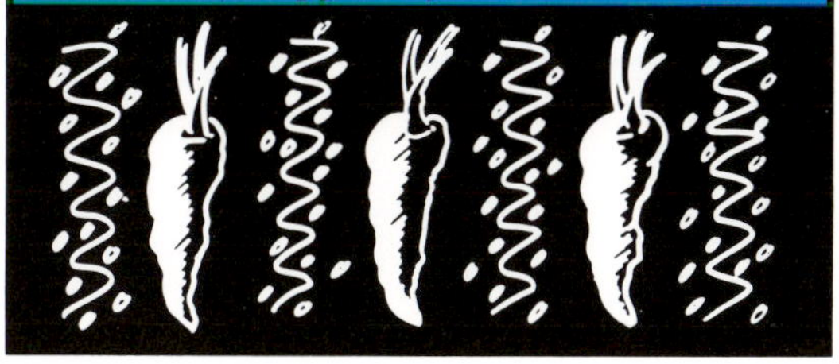

TOMATO, CARROT AND RICE SOUP

Ingredients
1 tbsp oil
2 tbsp/25g/1oz butter
2 onions, peeled and finely chopped
2 stalks celery, washed
2 carrots, scraped
3 cups/2 × 425g/15oz canned peeled tomatoes
¼ tsp oregano
1 tbsp tomato purée (tomato paste)
1 bouquet garni
1 bay leaf
2½ cups/600ml/1pt stock
1 tsp sugar
salt and freshly ground pepper
¼ cup/50g/2oz long-grain rice
Garnish
1 tbsp chopped parsley

To prepare

♦ Heat the oil and butter in a large saucepan. Add the onions and allow to cook over a low heat until translucent.

♦ Remove the strings from the round side of the celery stalks and chop finely. Add to the onions.

♦ Grate the carrots and add to the vegetables. Mix well. Pour in the tomatoes with the oregano, tomato purée, bouquet garni, bay leaf, sugar and half the stock.

♦ Bring to the boil and simmer for 15 minutes.

♦ Blend the soup or rub through a wide-meshed sieve.

♦ Season well. Add remaining stock and the rice. Cover and simmer until the rice is cooked.

Garnish with chopped parsley.

Serves 4

VEGETABLE BROTH

If you are making the stock for this broth, a ham bone gives an excellent flavour and any meat on the bone can be added to the soup.

Ingredients
4 tbsp/50g/2oz butter
2 onions, peeled and finely chopped
2 carrots, scraped and diced
1 small turnip, peeled and diced
2 stalks of celery, washed
4½ cups/1l/1¾pt water or stock
2 tbsp tomato purée (tomato paste)
1 bouquet garni
1 bay leaf
½ tsp mixed herbs
¼ cup/50g/2oz long-grain rice
2 leeks, washed and chopped
salt and freshly ground pepper
¼ small cabbage, finely shredded
1 tbsp chopped parsley

To prepare

♦ Prepare all the vegetables.

♦ Melt the butter and toss the onion, celery, carrots and turnip in the saucepan. Stir over a low heat for about 4 minutes.

♦ Add the water or stock to the vegetables. Then add the tomato purée, bouquet garni, bay leaf and mixed herbs. Bring to the boil. Add rice and simmer for 15 minutes.

♦ Add leeks and seasoning and continue cooking for a further 5 minutes.

♦ Finally add the finely shredded cabbage and cook for a further 5 minutes or until the rice is cooked. Toss in chopped parsley and serve.

Variation

Add peas or sliced green beans with 2½ cups or a 425-g/15-oz can of tomatoes and the leeks to make a really thick minestrone soup which can be served with grated cheese.

Serves 4 to 6

DOLMADES

Extra rolls may be kept in the freezer for future use as it is more economical to make up a whole packet of vine leaves.

Ingredients

1 package (vacuum-packed) preserved vine leaves
2 tbsp vegetable oil
2 large onions, peeled and finely chopped
1 cup/225g/8oz risotto rice
1½ tbsp/25g/1oz pine nuts, chopped
4 tbsp freshly chopped parsley
1 tsp mint
2 tbsp currants
salt and freshly ground pepper
1 cup/175g/6oz cooked minced (ground) lamb (optional)
1¼ cups/300ml/½pt water
⅔ cup/150ml/¼pt salad oil
juice of 2 lemons
oven temperature 170°C/325°F/Gas 3

To prepare

♦ Rinse the vine leaves and blanch in water for 2 minutes or treat according to the instructions on the packet.

♦ Heat the vegetable oil in a pan on a low heat and cook the finely chopped onions for about 3 minutes until they become transparent.

♦ Add the risotto rice and stir gently. Add the chopped pine nuts, parsley, mint, currants and seasoning.

♦ Gradually stir in 1¼ cup/300ml/½pt boiling water. Cover and cook for about 10 minutes until the water is absorbed. If you are using minced lamb stir it in at this stage.

♦ Smooth the leaves on a board and place 1 teaspoon of stuffing in the centre of each one. Fold the stem end up and the sides in, and roll firmly.

♦ Line an ovenproof dish with any leaves which are not suitable for rolling and pack the rolls tightly into the dish seam-side down. Finish one layer and sprinkle with salad oil and lemon juice.

♦ Continue packing layers until leaves are used up sprinkling each with oil and lemon juice. Cover with foil and weight with empty baking tins to keep rolls in shape.

♦ Cook for 1 hour. Then remove from the heat. Allow to cool and excess liquid will be absorbed. Chill before serving.

To serve

Place in a serving dish and garnish with lemon wedges. These delicious little rolls are Greek in origin and are usually served with a bowl of chilled yoghurt.

Makes approximately 60

SUMMER AVOCADO

Ingredients
2 ripe avocados
1 tbsp lemon juice
2 grapefruit
1 small lettuce
¼ cucumber
⅔ cup/150ml/¼pt Vinaigrette Dressing (see page 28)
¾ cup/100g/4oz cooked prawns (shrimp)
⅓ cup/50g/2oz yellow long-grain rice, cooked
1 yellow pepper, seeded
salt and freshly ground pepper

To prepare

♦ Peel the avocados. Cut them in half and remove the stones. Cut the flesh in slices and pour on the lemon juice to prevent discoloration.

♦ Using a small sharp knife, cut a slice from the grapefruit exposing the flesh. Cut round in strips removing all the white pith.

♦ When the grapefruit are peeled and showing no pith, cut into each section between the membranes of each slice. At the end you will have segments of grapefruit without skin. Squeeze the juice of the membranes by hand over the fruit.

♦ Line the dishes with washed, drained lettuce leaves and cucumber slices.

♦ Pour some of the Vinaigrette Dressing over the grapefruit.

♦ Mix the cooked prawns with the rice and dressing.

♦ Cut the yellow pepper in thin strips. Retaining some for garnishing, chop the remainder and mix with the rice and prawns. Season well.

♦ Arrange the prawn and rice mixture in the dishes on the cucumber and lettuce.

To serve

Top with sliced avocado and grapefruit. Garnish with pepper rings.

Serves 4

AVOCADO FISH

Ingredients
2 avocados
juice of 1 lemon
¾ cup/100g/4oz cooked prawns (shrimp) or tuna fish
⅔ cup/150ml/¼pt natural yoghurt
1 tsp cumin powder
1 clove garlic, crushed
¼ cup/50g/2oz long-grain rice
Garnish
rind of lemon
¼ tsp paprika

To prepare

♦ Slice the avocados lengthwise. Remove the stones. Remove some of the flesh and sprinkle lemon juice into the shells and on to the flesh.

♦ Mix the prawns or tuna fish with the diced avocado flesh.

♦ In a small bowl mix the yoghurt, cumin and crushed garlic. Stir well. Add the cooked rice and the avocado and fish mixture.

♦ Arrange the filling in the avocado shells.

To serve

Garnish with lemon rind and paprika.

Serves 4

BLUE CHEESE RICE QUICHE

Ingredients
Shortcrust pastry
1 cup + 2 tbsp/100g/4oz plain flour (all-purpose flour)
a pinch of salt
2 tbsp/25g/1oz butter or margarine
2 tbsp/25g/1oz white fat
1½ tbsp cold water
Filling
⅓ cup/50g/2oz cooked long-grain rice
¾ cup/75g/3oz blue cheese, crumbled
2 eggs
2 tbsp single cream (cereal cream)
salt and freshly ground pepper
a pinch of cayenne pepper
¼ tsp dry mustard
2 tsp chopped parsley
oven temperatures 200°C/400°F/Gas 6 180°C/350°F/Gas 4

To prepare

♦ Make up the pastry by sieving the flour and salt into a bowl. Add the fat in small lumps and rub in with the finger tips until the mixture resembles fine breadcrumbs. Add the water, a few drops at a time, and mix to a firm dough. Rest in the refrigerator for 15 minutes.

♦ Roll the pastry out in a neat circle to fit a 17.5-cm/7-in flan ring (pie plate). Lift the pastry on to the rolling pin and over the ring. Then ease it in to avoid stretching. Trim the top with the rolling pin. Line with greaseproof paper (waxed paper) and some baking beans. Bake in the preheated oven for 15 minutes at the higher temperature. Remove the paper and baking beans and cook for a further 5 minutes. Allow to cool slightly.

♦ Arrange the rice in the bottom of the flan. Mix the crumbled blue cheese with the rice. Beat the eggs in a cup. Add the single cream and seasonings. Pour over the rice and cheese. Sprinkle with chopped parsley. Bake for 20 minutes at the lower temperature until set and golden.

Serves 4

MAYONNAISE

Ingredients

2 egg yolks

1¼ cups/250ml/scant ½pt salad or olive oil

½ tsp salt

a pinch of dry mustard

1 tbsp wine vinegar or lemon juice

To prepare

♦ Beat the egg yolks together for a minute in a bowl which has been warmed but is completely dry.

♦ Making sure the oil is not too cold, add drop by drop, stirring with a wooden spoon or small wire whisk.

♦ When the mixture begins to thicken the oil can be added more quickly until a thick creamy sauce is obtained.

♦ Add the seasoning to the vinegar and add to the mixture slowly, as too much vinegar will thin the mayonnaise.

Makes 1¼ cups/300ml/½pt

BLENDER MAYONNAISE

Ingredients

1 whole egg

¼ tsp dried mustard

salt and freshly ground pepper

1 tbsp lemon juice or vinegar

1¼ cups/250ml/scant ½pt salad or olive oil

To prepare

♦ Break the egg into the blender. Add the mustard and seasoning. Blend until the egg is foamy, which is about 3 seconds.

♦ Add the lemon juice or vinegar and blend for a further 10 seconds.

♦ Switch the blender to high and pour the oil into the centre of the mixture in a continuous, very thin stream.

♦ After about half the oil has been added the sauce will begin to thicken. Continue to add the oil in a thin stream. If the sauce becomes too thick, add a little more vinegar or lemon juice and finally taste for seasoning.

Makes 1¼ cups/300ml/½pt

Variations

For Herb Mayonnaise add 3 tablespoons chives, some basil, oregano, parsley, tarragon or chervil or, if preferred, a mixture of green herbs to 1¼ cups/300ml/½pt Blender Mayonnaise.

For Green Mayonnaise add 2 tablespoons sieved or blended spinach, 1 tablespoon finely chopped green spring onion (scallion) tops, and 1 tablespoon finely chopped parsley to 1¼ cups/300ml/½pt Blender Mayonnaise.

VINAIGRETTE DRESSING

The proportion for this dressing is usually 3 times the amount of oil to vinegar but you can experiment and make a mixture to suit your personal taste. If you run out of vinegar, lemon juice can be used instead.

Ingredients

1½ tbsp wine vinegar

2 tsp lemon juice

salt and freshly ground pepper

a pinch of dry mustard (optional)

6 tbsp oil

1–2 tbsp chopped parsley, chives, tarragon or basil

To prepare

♦ Put all the ingredients in a clean, dry, screw-top jar and shake vigorously for about ½ minute to blend well.

♦ Taste for seasoning and shake again before use. Do not store for more than a few days as dressing is best when fresh.

As salad vegetables are so expensive now, serve dressing separately so that uneaten salad can be used again.

Makes approximately ⅔ cup/150ml/¼pt

BEAN SPROUT AND RICE SALAD

Ingredients

approx ¾ cup/175-g/6-oz can bean sprouts
1 tbsp vegetable oil
1 tbsp soya sauce
1 small piece of root ginger, finely chopped
salt and freshly ground pepper
6 spring onions (scallions)
⅔ cup/100g/4oz cooked long-grain rice
4 tbsp salad oil
2 tbsp lemon juice
½ tsp sugar
4 slices of Chinese leaves (Chinese cabbage or 'Bok Choy')

To prepare

♦ Drain the can of bean sprouts. Heat the vegetable oil in a small saucepan. Toss in the bean sprouts with the soya sauce and finely chopped ginger. Stir well. Cover and cook for 3 minutes on a low heat.

♦ Turn the bean sprouts into a bowl and allow to cool. Season well.

♦ Chop the spring onions into small pieces and add to the cooled shoots. Retain a few pieces for garnish.

♦ Stir in the rice.

♦ Mix the salad oil with the lemon juice in a screw-top jar.

♦ Arrange the Chinese leaves in the bottom of the salad bowl. Shake the oil and lemon juice dressing and pour over the bean shoots and rice. Mix well and arrange in the salad bowl.

To serve

Garnish with a few rings of chopped spring onions.

Serves 4

HAM AND ASPARAGUS SALAD

This is a quick and easy buffet dish or it can be served as a starter or easy lunch.

Ingredients
1⅓ cups/225g/8oz long-grain rice, cooked
⅔ cup/150ml/¼pt Vinaigrette Dressing (see page 32)
8 spring onions (scallions), washed
4 large slices of cooked ham
8 fresh or canned asparagus spears
a few lettuce leaves or watercress
⅔ cup/150ml/¼pt Mayonnaise (see page 32)

To prepare

♦ Mix the rice with the dressing in a bowl.

♦ Chop the spring onions finely and mix with the rice.

♦ Lay the ham flat on a board. Place 2 asparagus spears on the ham and roll up.

♦ Lay dressed rice on a bed of lettuce or surround with watercress. Arrange the rolls of ham on top and serve with mayonnaise in a jug.

Serves 4

WALDORF RICE SALAD

Ingredients

1 cup/225g/8oz long-grain rice
1 small onion, peeled and finely chopped
6 stalks celery, washed
4 spring onions (scallions), washed and chopped
½ cup/50g/2oz walnuts, chopped
1 red apple
1 green apple
⅔ cup/150ml/¼pt Mayonnaise (see page 32)
1 tbsp parsley
juice of 1 lemon

To prepare

♦ Cook the rice until fluffy, forking from time to time to separate the grains. Allow to cool.

♦ Add the finely chopped onion to the rice and mix well.

♦ Remove the strings from the celery stalks and chop finely. Add to the rice.

♦ Add the chopped spring onions and walnuts to the rice and mix well.

♦ Chop part of both apples into small cubes, sprinkle with lemon juice and mix with the rice salad, mayonnaise and parsley.

To serve

Decorate with remaining apple slices and walnut halves.

Serves 4

BARBECUE SAUCE

Ingredients

1 tbsp/14g/½oz butter
2 tbsp oil
1 large onion, peeled
1 green pepper, seeded
1 chilli (chili) pepper, seeded (optional)
2 stalks celery, washed
4 tomatoes or 1½ cups/450g/15oz-can peeled tomatoes
2 tbsp tomato purée (tomato paste)
2 tbsp sherry, wine vinegar or white wine
2½ cups/600ml/1pt water or stock
2 tbsp brown sugar
1 tsp Worcestershire sauce
1 tbsp flour
½ tsp mustard
salt and freshly ground pepper
a few drops of Tabasco or chilli (chili) sauce (optional)

To prepare

♦ Place the butter and oil in a saucepan to heat. Chop the onion, pepper, chilli pepper, celery and skinned tomatoes into very small dice and sauté for a few minutes in the oil and butter.

♦ Mix the purée, vinegar, water, sugar and Worcestershire sauce in a jug.

♦ Sprinkle the vegetables with the flour to absorb the excess fat. Pour on the liquid. Add the mustard and seasoning and simmer gently for 45 minutes. If a smooth sauce is required the vegetables can be sieved or blended.

♦ A few drops Tabasco or chilli sauce will give more fiery sauce. Add one drop and taste.

Makes 2½ cups/600ml/1pt

CURRY SAUCE

Curry is a matter of individual taste. If you like a mild curry reduce the powder by half.

Ingredients

2 onions, peeled
1 carrot, scraped
1 clove garlic, crushed
2 tbsp/25g/1oz butter
1 tbsp oil
1 tbsp curry powder
1 tbsp flour
3 cups/750ml/1¼pt stock or water
1 tsp tomato purée (tomato paste)
juice of ½ lemon
½ level tsp salt

To prepare

♦ Chop the onions finely. Grate the carrot. Melt the butter in a saucepan and add the oil. Put in the onion, garlic and carrot and cook gently for a few minutes.

♦ Raise the heat and sprinkle the curry powder and flour on the vegetables. Fry until all the fat is absorbed. Pour in the stock or water and stir well to ensure there is no sticking on the bottom of the pan. Add the tomato purée, lemon juice and salt.

♦ Simmer for 40 minutes.

To serve

This sauce goes well with meat, fish or chicken. It is also ideal for spicing up left-overs.

Makes 2½ cups/600ml/1pt

Variations

Add chopped apple and sultanas (white raisins) if you like them with curry.

To use as a vegetable curry add chopped vegetables, eg diced potato, aubergine (eggplant) or cauliflower, for the last 30 minutes of simmering.

SWEET AND SOUR SAUCE

Ingredients

1 onion, peeled
1 carrot, scraped
2 green peppers, seeded
1 level tbsp cornflour (cornstarch)
⅔ cup/150ml/¼pt wine vinegar
⅔ cup/150ml/¼pt tomato juice
¼ cup/50g/2oz sugar or 2 tbsp honey
salt and freshly ground pepper
3 tomatoes

To prepare

♦ Chop the onion into small dice. Cut the carrot into rings. Seed and dice the green peppers.

♦ Blend the cornflour with the wine vinegar and tomato juice. Pour into a saucepan. Add the sugar or honey and seasoning. Bring to the boil and simmer for 2 minutes, stirring from time to time.

♦ Add the chopped vegetables and cook for a further 5–10 minutes, until soft but not discoloured.

♦ Peel and chop the tomatoes. Add them at the end of the cooking time.

To serve

Accompany with pork, prawns (shrimp) or beef fondue.

Makes approximately 1¼ cups/300ml/½pt

Variation

Add a small can of chopped pineapples to the sauce.

SPICED RICE SALAD

Ingredients
1 cup/225g/8oz rice
1 tsp salt
1 tsp garam masala
1 tsp turmeric
1 bay leaf
2 tbsp/25g/1oz butter
1 clove garlic, crushed
1 onion, peeled and diced
⅓ cup/50g/2oz sultanas (white raisins)
1 green pepper, seeded, blanched and diced

Garnish
6 tbsp low-fat yoghurt
2 spring onions (scallions), washed

To prepare

♦ Cook the rice in boiling salted water with the garam masala, turmeric and bay leaf for about 15 minutes until tender.

♦ Meanwhile melt the butter and gently sweat the garlic and onion without browning for 5 minutes.

♦ Add the garlic and onion to the rice when it is cooked and allow it to cool.

♦ Stir in the sultanas and pepper.

To serve

Garnish with chopped spring onions. Stir in yoghurt before serving.

Serves 4

AUBERGINE (EGGPLANT) RICE CASSEROLE

Ingredients
2 aubergines (eggplant), washed
salt
juice of 1 lemon
1 cup/225g/8oz long-grain rice
4 tbsp vegetable oil
2 onions, peeled and finely chopped
2 cloves garlic, crushed
1 carrot, scraped and grated
1½ cups/425g/15oz canned peeled tomatoes
1 tsp tomato purée (tomato paste)
4 tbsp white wine
4 tbsp stock or water
1 tsp dried basil or 2 tsp freshly chopped basil leaves
2 cups/100g/4oz mushrooms, washed and sliced
4 tbsp grated cheese (preferably Parmesan)
oven temperature 180°C/350°F/Gas 4

To prepare

♦ Wash and cut the aubergines into thick slices lengthwise. Arrange on a tray lined with kitchen paper (kitchen towel). Sprinkle with a little salt and lemon juice. Allow to stand for 20–30 minutes.

♦ Cook the rice in 4½ cups/1l/1¾pt boiling salted water for 10 minutes. It should still be firm. Drain and toss in 2 tbsp/25g/1oz butter or oil. Place in the bottom of an oiled ovenproof dish or shallow casserole.

♦ Meanwhile heat half the oil in a saucepan and cook the onion and garlic gently for about 4 minutes over a low heat. Add the grated carrot and stir for a further 1 minute.

♦ Add the canned tomatoes, tomato purée, white wine and stock or water with the basil. Stir until the tomatoes are broken down. Simmer gently for 30 minutes.

♦ Pat the sliced aubergine dry with kitchen paper. Heat the remaining oil in a frying pan and fry slices on a medium heat until golden brown. Drain on absorbent kitchen paper.

♦ Place slices of aubergine over the rice. Season well. Add half the tomato sauce. Top with a further layer of aubergine and a layer of sliced mushrooms. Pour over the remaining tomato sauce.

♦ Sprinkle with grated cheese. Cook in the oven for 20–30 minutes until the rice is tender.

Serves 4

RICE À LA PROVENÇALE

This is a useful recipe to serve with many main dishes as there is no need to cook separate vegetables.

Ingredients

1 cup/225g/8oz long-grain rice
2½ cups/600ml/1pt water
½ tsp salt
4 tbsp oil
2 tbsp/25g/1oz butter
2 onions, peeled and finely chopped
2 cloves garlic, crushed
salt and freshly ground black pepper
2 red peppers, seeded and blanched
4 courgettes (zucchini), washed and thinly sliced
½ tsp basil
4 tbsp white wine
8 tomatoes, skinned and chopped

Garnish

1 tbsp chopped capers
2 hard-boiled (hard-cooked) eggs
8 green olives, stoned
2 tbsp chopped parsley or chervil

To prepare

♦ Cook the long-grain rice in 2½ cups/600ml/1pt water with ½ teaspoon salt, by bringing the water to the boil, adding the rice and stirring to separate the grains. Cover and simmer gently until the water has all been absorbed, which will take about 15 minutes.

♦ Heat the oil and butter and cook the onions over a low heat for about 4 minutes.

♦ Add the garlic. Dice the blanched peppers and add with the sliced courgettes, the basil and white wine. Stir gently until cooked for about 5 minutes. Lastly stir in the tomatoes. Gently fold in the cooked rice and season well.

♦ Add the chopped capers and turn into a heated serving dish.

To serve

Decorate with hard-boiled eggs, green olives and chopped herbs.

Serves 4

SAVOURY SPINACH AND RICE

Ingredients

450g/1lb frozen leaf spinach or 1kg/2lb fresh spinach, washed
2 tbsp/25g/1oz butter
1 tbsp oil
1 medium onion, peeled
1 leek, washed and trimmed
juice of ½ lemon
salt and freshly ground pepper
1 cup/225g/8oz long-grain rice
2½ cups/600ml/1pt water or stock
¼ tsp nutmeg
1 tbsp chopped parsley

Topping

1 tbsp natural yoghurt (optional)

To prepare

♦ Cook the frozen spinach as directed on the packet or, if thawed, simmer for a few minutes in 4 tablespoons water. Drain well in a colander, squeezing out excess moisture with the back of a wooden spoon. If using fresh spinach remove thick stems, tear into manageable pieces and cook in ½in/1.2cm boiling water for 4 minutes. Drain well.

♦ Heat the butter and oil over a low heat in a large saucepan. Slice the onion and leek finely and cook in the fat for 4–5 minutes. Sprinkle with lemon juice and seasoning.

♦ Add the long-grain rice and stir in with the vegetables. Add the boiling water or stock mixed with ½ teaspoon salt and pour over the rice and vegetables. Cover with a tight-fitting lid and simmer for 15 minutes. Remove the lid. Fluff the rice with a fork and add the spinach, nutmeg and chopped parsley. Mix with a fork, cover and reheat for 5 minutes.

To serve

Yoghurt may be spooned over. This dish goes well with meats or fish or it can be served simply as a vegetarian dish.

Serves 4

STUFFED TOMATOES

Ingredients
4 large tomatoes
⅓ cup/50g/2oz long-grain rice, cooked
salt and freshly ground pepper
2 tbsp oil
1 large onion, peeled
1 green pepper, seeded and sliced
1 chilli (chili) pepper, seeded and sliced
½ tsp curry powder (optional)
1½ tbsp/25g/1oz almonds, chopped
1 tsp chopped coriander or chopped parsley
⅓ cup/50g/2oz cooked minced (ground) beef, lamb or chicken
oven temperature 180°C/350°F/Gas 4

To prepare

♦ Remove the top of the tomatoes. Scoop out the centres into a bowl.

♦ Add the cooked long-grain rice. Season well.

♦ Heat the oil and fry the onion over a low heat for 3 minutes. Add the sliced pepper and chilli. Sprinkle with the curry powder and continue cooking for 2 minutes. Add the chopped almonds.

♦ Finally sprinkle in the chopped coriander or parsley. Add the meat and mix well.

♦ Fill each tomato with the rice mixture. Brush the tomatoes with oil. Then cook in the oven for about 15 minutes.

Serves 4

STUFFED COURGETTES (ZUCCHINI)

Ingredients

4 large courgettes (zucchini)
1 onion, peeled
1 red pepper, seeded
1 green pepper, seeded
4 tbsp vegetable oil
1 clove garlic, crushed
⅔ cup/100g/4oz cooked long-grain rice
⅔ cup/100g/4oz cooked chicken (optional)
2 tbsp cooked sweetcorn (corn)
¼ tsp cumin
½ tsp garam masala
salt and freshly ground pepper
⅔ cup/150ml/¼pt sour cream
1 tbsp chopped parsley
oven temperature 180°C/350°F/Gas 4

To prepare

♦ Wash the courgettes and cut a thin slice lengthwise across the top of each. Scoop out the flesh and chop into small pieces. Cut a small slice off the bottom if any of the courgettes are tipping over when laid flat.

♦ Prepare the vegetables by dicing the onion and peppers. Heat the oil in a frying pan and cook the onion for 3 minutes. Then add the peppers and garlic. Cook for a further 3 minutes.

♦ Add the rice and stir well. If you are using chicken dice and add at this stage. Sprinkle in the sweetcorn and the seasonings over a low heat and mix for 1 minute.

♦ Brush the courgette shells with oil and fill with the rice mixture. Pour the sour cream over and bake in the oven for 20 minutes.

To serve

Sprinkle with chopped parsley.

Serves 4

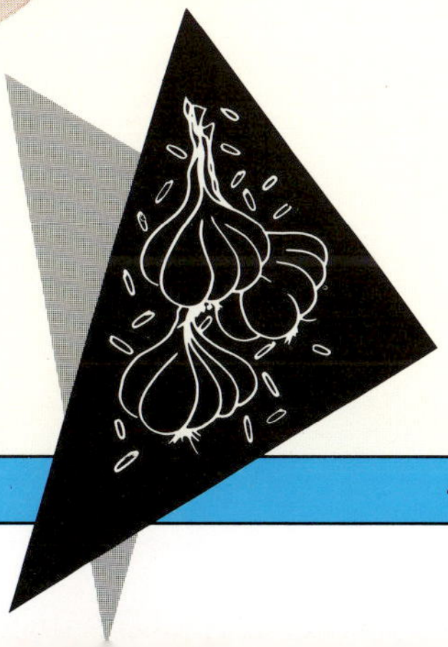

SAVOURY RICE RING WITH VEGETABLE CURRY

Ingredients
1 cup/225g/8oz basmati or long-grain rice
3 tbsp oil
1 onion, peeled and finely chopped
¼ green pepper, washed and seeded
1 red pepper, washed and seeded
salt and freshly ground pepper
¼ tsp garam masala
Vegetable Curry
1 large onion, peeled
1 clove garlic, crushed
2.5cm/1in fresh root ginger
1 level tbsp mild curry powder
¾ cup/200g/7oz canned peeled tomatoes
1 carrot, scraped
1 potato, peeled
1 small cauliflower
2 tbsp oil
1 tsp ground cumin
1 tbsp lemon juice
1 bay leaf
1 cup/50g/2oz mushrooms
oven temperature 180°C/350°F/Gas 4

To prepare

♦ Rinse the rice well. Partly cook for about 10 minutes after it has come to the boil (see page 11). Rinse off excess liquid with cold water. Drain well.

♦ Place 2 tablespoons oil in a frying pan and cook the onion over a low heat for 3 minutes. Add half the green and red pepper, cut into small dice, and continue cooking for a further 3 minutes. Tip the rice into the pan with the vegetables. Mix well with seasoning and the garam masala.

♦ Oil a ring mould. Mix the remaining oil with the rice mixture and place it in the ring mould. Cook in the oven for 15 minutes.

♦ Meanwhile chop half the onion into thin rings.

♦ Make a curry paste by chopping the remaining half of the onion and blending it with the garlic, root ginger and curry powder, mixed with 2 tablespoons tomato juice.

♦ Cut the carrot into rings and dice the potato. Boil in a little salted water for 5 minutes. Drain and retain the vegetable water.

♦ Cut the cauliflower into florets and steep in cold water.

♦ Heat the oil and fry the onion rings for 3 minutes. Remove to another saucepan.

♦ Fry the curry paste on a fairly high heat until brown. Rinse the pan into the onion saucepan with the remaining juice of the tomatoes and 1¼ cups/300ml/½pt vegetable water.

♦ Add the carrots, the potato, the remaining halves of the red and green peppers, the cauliflower florets, ground cumin, lemon juice, salt, bay leaf and chopped tomatoes.

♦ Bring to the boil and simmer for 25 minutes, stirring well to mix the ingredients and to avoid sticking. Add the mushrooms and allow to simmer for a further 5 minutes. Remove the bay leaf and taste for seasoning.

♦ After removing the rice from the oven leave for a few minutes to shrink. Gently turn the rice ring out of the mould on to a heated serving plate. Pour the vegetable curry into the centre of the ring.

To serve

Turn excess curry on to a separate dish and serve with other suitable curry accompaniments, such as poppadoms and mango chutney.

Serves 4

STUFFED AUBERGINES (EGGPLANT)

Ingredients

- ¼ cup/50g/2oz brown rice
- 2 even-sized large aubergines (eggplant)
- 2 tbsp/25g/1oz butter
- 2 tbsp oil
- 1 large onion, peeled and finely chopped
- 1 clove garlic, crushed
- 1 cup/225g/8oz minced (ground) lamb
- ¾ cup/200g/7oz canned peeled tomatoes, drained

Sauce

- 1½ tbsp/20g/¾oz butter
- 1 tbsp/20g/¾oz flour
- 1¼ cups/300ml/½pt milk
- salt and freshly ground pepper
- 1 cup/50g/2oz mushrooms, washed and sliced

Topping

- ½ cup/50g/2oz grated cheese
- oven temperature 180°C/350°F/Gas 4

To prepare

♦ Cook the brown rice in 1¼ cups/300ml/½pt water (see page 11) until almost tender.

♦ Cut the aubergines in half lengthwise. Scoop out the centre flesh to make room for the filling. Dice the flesh.

♦ Heat the butter and oil in a frying pan and cook the onions until translucent over a low heat. Add the diced aubergines after a few minutes and cook for a further 2 minutes. Remove with a slotted spoon onto a plate.

♦ Add the garlic to the remaining fat in the pan and then gradually add the minced lamb and cook until browned. Remove from the heat and mix with the drained tomatoes and other vegetables.

♦ Make the sauce by melting the butter in a saucepan, adding the flour and stirring over a low heat without browning to make a roux. Gradually add the milk stirring or whisking until smooth. Add the sliced mushrooms.

♦ Fill the aubergines with the rice and lamb mixture which should be well seasoned. Top with the mushroom sauce and finally with the grated cheese.

♦ Place the aubergines in a roasting pan with 1.2-cm/½-in water in the bottom, and bake for 40 minutes.

Serves 4

STUFFED BAKED CABBAGE SUPPER

Ingredients
8 large cabbage leaves
stuffing
1 tbsp oil
1 large onion
½ cup/125g/4oz long-grain rice
1 cup/225g/8oz minced (ground) beef
salt and freshly ground pepper
1 tsp Worcestershire sauce
Quick Tomato Sauce
4 spring onions (scallions), washed and chopped
1½ cups/425g/15oz canned peeled tomatoes
⅔ cup/150ml/¼pt beef stock
1 tsp dried basil
1 bay leaf
bouquet garni
2 drops Tabasco sauce
½ tsp sugar
½ tsp lemon juice
2 tsp tomato purée (tomato paste)
1 tsp cornflour (cornstarch)
2 tbsp water
oven temperature 180°C/350°F/Gas 4

To prepare

♦ Place the cabbage leaves in a saucepan with enough cold water to cover them and bring them to the boil. Drain and place on a board.

♦ Heat the oil in a frying pan. Add the onion and cook for 3 minutes over a low heat.

♦ Put the rice to cook in 1¼ cups/300ml/½pt boiling water with ½ teaspoon salt. After it comes back to the boil, cook for 10 minutes. Rinse with cold water and drain well.

♦ Add the beef to the onions, and break-down into small pieces with a fork while allowing the meat to brown. Stir constantly until the minced beef grains are separate and browned. Allow to cool. Add seasoning and Worcestershire sauce. Mix well.

♦ Mix the beef and onions with the undercooked rice.

♦ Meanwhile make up the Quick Tomato Sauce by adding the chopped spring onions to the blended or sieved tomatoes in a saucepan. Add all ingredients except the cornflour and water. Bring to the boil and simmer for 20 minutes. After 15 minutes mix the cornflour and water and add a little hot sauce. Pour the mixture into the sauce and heat until it slightly thickens.

♦ Cut any large thick stems from the bottom of the cabbage leaves and divide the stuffing between the 8 leaves. Fold each one into a parcel and secure with a cocktail stick (toothpick). Place in a casserole or ovenproof dish and pour over the tomato sauce. Cook in the oven for 25 minutes.

♦ Remove the bouquet garni, bay leaf and cocktail sticks before serving.

Serves 4

SPICY OKRA

Ingredients
3½–4 cups/450g/1lb okra
4 tbsp oil
1 large onion, peeled and chopped
1 chilli (chili) pepper, seeded and chopped
2 tsp cumin seeds
2 tsp coriander seeds
2 cloves garlic, peeled and crushed
2 tomatoes, peeled and chopped or approx ¾ cup/175g/6oz canned peeled tomatoes
¼ tsp salt
¼ tsp sugar
2 tbsp lemon juice
⅔ cup/50ml/¼pt water

To prepare

♦ Remove the little end pieces of the okra. Heat 3 tablespoons oil in a frying pan and fry until golden for 2 minutes. Remove from the pan.

♦ Blend 1 tablespoon oil, the onion, chilli, cumin and coriander seeds with the garlic in a food processor or blender. Add a few drops of water if too thick.

♦ Heat the oil again in the pan and fry the paste on a fairly high heat for about 2 minutes. Lower the heat. Add the okra, chopped tomatoes salt, sugar and lemon juice. Add the water and simmer for 10–15 minutes.

To serve

Accompany with curry dishes and rice.

Serves 4

SPANISH RICE

Ingredients
1 cup/225g/8oz long-grain rice
2½ cups/600ml/1pt stock or water
1 tsp salt
½ tsp turmeric
2 tbsp vegetable oil
½ cup/125g/4oz chicken livers, trimmed and chopped
1 onion, peeled and finely chopped
6 tomatoes, peeled and chopped or 1½ cups/425g/15oz canned peeled tomatoes
salt and freshly ground pepper
¼ tsp sugar
2 red peppers, seeded, chopped and blanched
½ cup/125g/4oz-pkt thawed petits pois (peas)
¾ cup/125g/4oz cooked prawns (shrimp)
1 tbsp chopped parsley

To prepare

♦ Cook the long-grain rice with boiling water or stock to which the salt and turmeric has been added. Cook by absorption method (see page 9).

♦ Meanwhile heat the oil in a frying pan, and over a medium heat fry the chopped chicken livers until golden brown. Turn the heat down and add the onion. Cook, stirring well, for 4 minutes. Add the tomatoes, salt, pepper, sugar and chopped peppers. Stir gently.

♦ Add the thawed peas and prawns. Heat through in the vegetable mixture and mix in the warmed rice.

To serve

Turn out into a dish and serve hot. A little butter may be added if you like.

Serves 4

DAL

Ingredients

- 1 cup/200g/7oz red lentils
- 3¾ cups/900ml/1½pt water
- ¼ turmeric
- 1 tsp salt
- 3 tbsp oil
- 1 medium onion, peeled
- 2 cloves garlic, crushed
- 1 tsp ground coriander
- ½ tsp cumin
- ¼ tsp chilli (chili) powder (optional)
- 1 tbsp chopped coriander or parsley

To prepare

♦ Wash the lentils and remove any discoloured seeds, pour into a saucepan with the water. Bring to the boil and turn heat to simmering for 5 minutes. Skim the surface with a slotted spoon.

♦ Add the salt and turmeric to the lentils and cook for 45–60 minutes until the lentils are tender.

♦ Cut a few thin rings of onion and retain. Dice the remainder of the onion finely.

♦ Heat the oil in a frying pan on a high heat and fry the onion rings for garnish. Remove from the pan. Turn heat to medium, add chopped onion and garlic and cook for 2 minutes.

♦ Sprinkle with coriander, cumin and chilli. Stir the mixture into the onion and cook for 1 minute.

♦ Pour into the cooked lentils and mix well. Add chopped herbs, and serve topped with onion rings.

Serves 4

Serve with rice and curried meats or chicken.

SPICED MUSHROOMS

Ingredients

- 3 tablespoons oil
- 1 onion, peeled
- 2 cloves garlic, crushed
- 1 tsp garam masala
- ½ tsp ground cumin
- ½ tsp ground coriander
- 2 tsp flour
- ½ tsp mild curry powder
- 1¼ cups/300ml/½pt stock or water
- ½ tsp salt
- 2 carrots, scraped
- 1 potato, peeled
- 4 cups/225g/8oz mushrooms, washed
- 1½ cups/425g/15oz canned peeled tomatoes
- 1 tbsp chopped coriander or parsley

To prepare

♦ Chop the onion finely and place 1 teaspoon into a small bowl. Mix with the crushed garlic, garam masala, cumin, coriander and flour and curry powder to a thick paste with a little of the stock.

♦ Heat the remaining oil on a low heat and cook the rest of the onion for 3 minutes. Remove to a saucepan or casserole.

♦ Turn the heat up for the frying pan and fry the paste in the oil for a few minutes. Gradually whisk in the stock.

♦ Cut the carrots into thin rings and the potato into small dice and cook in a saucepan of salted water for 5 minutes after the vegetables come to the boil. Drain.

♦ Slice or dice the mushrooms, add to the stock. Transfer the stock to the onion, add the carrots, potatoes and tomatoes. Mix well and simmer for 25 minutes or until vegetables are tender.

♦ Sprinkle with parsley or coriander. Serve with rice, sambals (see page 63) and if liked a meat or chicken curry.

Serves 4

Ritzy Meat

Mexican chilli (chili)

BEEFBURGERS (HAMBURGERS) WITH SPICY TOMATO SAUCE

Ingredients
2 cups/450g/1lb lean minced (ground) beef
1 onion, peeled and finely chopped
1 green pepper, seeded
2 tbsp fresh breadcrumbs
1 egg
1 tsp Worcestershire sauce
salt and freshly ground pepper
Spicy tomato sauce
1 tsp oil
1 onion, peeled and finely chopped
1 chilli (chili) pepper seeded (optional)
1 clove garlic, crushed
1 carrot, scraped and grated
¾ cup/200g/7oz canned peeled tomatoes
⅔ cup/150ml/¼pt stock or water
1 bay leaf
½ tsp oregano
1 cup/225g/8oz long-grain rice (see page 11)

To prepare

♦ Place the meat in a bowl with the very finely chopped onion.

♦ Chop the pepper into very small dice. If you prefer, both onion and pepper can be chopped in a blender.

♦ Add the breadcrumbs. Mix with a beaten egg and add the Worcestershire sauce and seasoning.

♦ Divide the mixture into 8 pieces and shape into rounds. A scone or pastry cutter is ideal for this purpose. Place on a tray in the refrigerator to chill while making the sauce.

♦ To make the sauce heat the oil in a saucepan and cook over a low heat for 4 minutes. Add the garlic and grated carrot. Stir well and then add remaining ingredients. Season well. Simmer for at least 20 minutes on a low heat.

♦ Brush the beefburgers over with oil and grill (broil) under a high heat for 4 minutes each side. If you like beef well cooked give the burgers a further 3 minutes.

♦ Cook rice as directed on page 11. Serve with the beefburgers and sauce.

Serves 4

STUFFED BEEF ROLLS

Ingredients

4 slices lean shoulder steak
⅔ cup/125g/4oz savoury rice stuffing (see page 17)
2 tbsp vegetable oil
1 onion, peeled and sliced
1 clove garlic, crushed
1 tbsp flour
1 bay leaf
salt and freshly ground pepper
1 bouquet garni
1 sprig parsley
⅔ cup/150ml/¼pt red wine
1¼ cups/300ml/½pt beef stock
oven temperature 180°C/350°F/Gas 4

To prepare

♦ Lay the thin slices of beef on a board and trim off surplus fat. Cut into suitable sizes for rolls, about 7cm/2½in.

♦ Place 1 tablespoon rice stuffing on each slice. Roll tightly and secure with string or a wooden cocktail stick (toothpick).

♦ Heat the oil in a frying pan and brown the rolls on each side. Place in an ovenproof casserole. Retain frying pan on lower heat.

♦ Fry onion and garlic in remaining oil in frying pan for 3 minutes. Sprinkle with flour and brown slightly. Add the bay leaf, seasoning, bouquet garni, parsley and red wine. Stir well, then add the stock. Cook for 5 minutes.

♦ Pour the sauce from the frying pan on top of the rolls and cook in the oven for 1–1½ hours or until meat is tender. Remove bouquet garni and bay leaf.

To serve

Serve with a crisp green vegetable, such as green beans, broccoli or a mixture of carrots and peas.

Serves 4–6

THAI BEEF WITH SPINACH

Ingredients
700g/1½lb chuck steak
1¼ cups/300ml/½pt Coconut Milk (see page 62)
1 tsp brown sugar
1 tbsp soya sauce
1 tbsp mixed chopped nuts
2 cloves garlic, crushed
1 onion, peeled
2.5cm/1in fresh root ginger
2 fresh chilli peppers (chilis), seeded
salt and freshly ground pepper, seeded
juice of ½ lemon
1 tbsp cornflour (cornstarch)
450g/1lb frozen spinach or 1kg/2lb fresh spinach
4 tbsp yoghurt

To prepare

♦ Trim off excess fat from the meat, and cut into thin strips.

♦ Put the coconut milk, sugar, nuts and soya sauce into a saucepan. Mix the beef with these ingredients and bring to the boil. Immediately the mixture bubbles, turn the heat down and allow to simmer for about 10 minutes.

♦ In a blender or food processor make a paste with the garlic, onion, fresh ginger, chilli peppers, a little salt and lemon juice. Mix this paste with the cornflour and a little cold water. Add some of the hot liquid from the beef to the mixture before stirring into the beef. Cover and simmer gently for about 30–40 minutes until meat is cooked.

♦ Cook the spinach as directed on the packet if using frozen. For fresh spinach wash and remove large stems and cook in a small amount of boiling salted water for about 5 minutes. Drain cooking water into a bowl and use to adjust sauce if it has reduced too much. Arrange drained spinach in a hot serving dish.

♦ Put beef onto the spinach and trickle yoghurt on top.

♦ Serve with plain boiled rice (see page 10) .

Serves 4

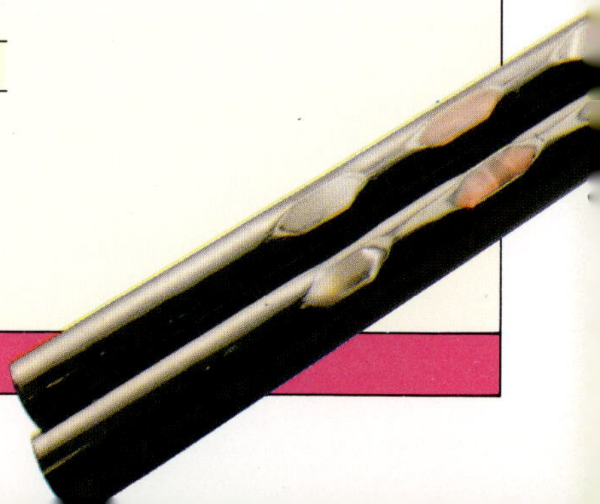

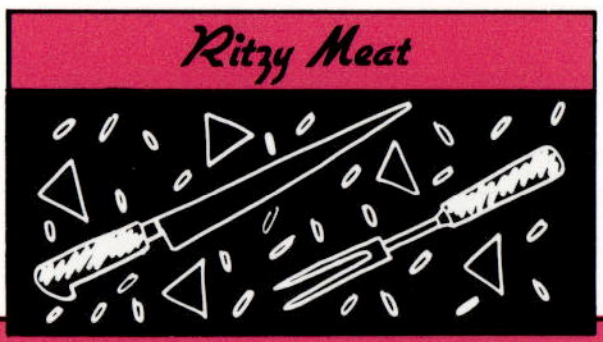

CURRY POWDER

Many of the delicious recipes accompanying rice from the south of India, Sri Lanka and Indonesia use coconut milk as a stock. It is worth mentioning that coconut milk is made from coconut but it is not the liquid inside the fresh coconut. This liquid is the water and is either discarded or can be used as a drink. The milk is made from the grated flesh or dried desiccated (shredded) coconut. It is much easier to grate the coconut flesh in a food processor or blender.

COCONUT MILK

Ingredients

1 coconut or 1 cup/225g/8oz desiccated coconut

To prepare

♦ Hit the coconut in the middle with a hammer. With luck it will break into two halves. Drain the water but do not use for cooking. Taste the flesh to make sure it is sweet. Remove the white flesh from the brown skin with a knife. Grate by hand or in a blender or food processor. The freshly grated coconut can be made into milk or can be frozen in small packets for future use.

♦ Cover the grated coconut with approximately 1¼ cups/300ml/½pt of boiling water and allow to stand for 1 hour. Strain the liquid and put the coconut in muslin (cheesecloth) or a clean J-Cloth and squeeze out all the liquid. Soak the coconut again for about 12 hours and then strain again.

♦ To make milk with dried coconut pour 2½ cups/600ml/1pt of boiling water over the dried coconut and leave to soak for 24 hours.

Makes 2½ cups/600ml/1pt

Rice is the natural partner for spicy food and curry springs to mind immediately rice is mentioned.

There are many excellent blended curry powders on the market for those who want easy spicy food. However it is now possible to buy many fresh spices and seeds, and it is interesting and fun to experiment with these to produce a blend of your own. Keep small amounts of spices in containers with air-tight lids. If buying ready-mixed powder read the packet carefully to make sure it is suitable for your taste, either mild or hot.

Here is a basic recipe for a mild curry powder which you can make at home. A small coffee grinder is most suitable for making this mixture, since grinding by hand is a tedious process.

MILD MIX CURRY

Ingredients

⅔ cup/100g/4oz coriander seeds
⅔ cup/100g/4oz cumin seeds
3 black peppercorns
2 cardamom pods
2 tsp mustard seeds
3 tbsp/50g/2oz dried root ginger
6 tbsp/75g/3oz ground turmeric

To prepare

♦ Grind all the ingredients together except the ginger and turmeric. Gradually add these. Store in an air-tight jar.

HOT MIX CURRY

Ingredients

Mild Mix Curry
½–1 tsp chilli (chili) powder
1 tsp mace
1 tsp poppy seeds
½ tsp allspice

To prepare

♦ Add the Mild Mix Curry to the other ingredients. Try out the amount of chilli (chili) to ensure that the mixture is not too fiery.

This is the name given to the side dishes which accompany Indian and Pakistani food. They are mainly prepared with fresh vegetables and they add great variety and colour to spiced dishes, especially rice and curry.

TOMATO SAMBAL

Ingredients

2–3 tomatoes, skinned and sliced

1 small onion, peeled and thinly sliced

2 tsp fresh coriander, chopped or ½ tsp dried (if unobtainable use chopped parsley)

2 tsp lemon juice

¼ tsp sugar

salt and freshly ground pepper

To prepare

♦ Arrange rings of tomatoes and onions overlapping on a small plate.

♦ Sprinkle the other ingredients on each layer.

CUCUMBER RAITA

Ingredients

1 cucumber

salt

1 tbsp lemon juice

1 tsp cumin

1 clove garlic, crushed (optional)

1 tsp chopped coriander (optional)

1¼ cups/300ml/½pt natural yoghurt

To prepare

♦ Cut the cucumber. Peel in strips leaving a little green. Either chop into small dice or grate with a coarse grater.

♦ Add the other ingredients.

♦ Allow to stand for 30 minutes in the refrigerator to chill.

RED CABBAGE AND LEMON JUICE WITH ONION

Ingredients

¼ red cabbage

1 onion, peeled

2 tbsp lemon juice

salt and pepper

To prepare

♦ Shred the cabbage and thinly slice the onion. Arrange in layers on a small dish.

♦ Season each layer of onion and cabbage. Pour the lemon juice over.

BANANA AND COCONUT

Ingredients

2 bananas

2 tbsp lemon juice

2 tbsp desiccated (shredded) coconut or freshly grated coconut

To prepare

♦ Peel the bananas and cut into slices.

♦ Sprinkle with lemon juice and coconut.

GREEN PEPPER SAMBAL

Ingredients

2 green peppers, seeded

1 onion, peeled and thinly sliced

¼ tsp garam masala

To prepare

♦ Slice the peppers in thin slices and arrange in a dish with the onion rings.

♦ Sprinkle each layer with garam masala.

BEEF SATÉ

Ingredients
2 spring onions (scallions), washed
2.5cm/1in fresh root ginger, grated
2 cloves garlic, crushed
8 cardamom pods
1 tsp cumin seeds
1 tsp coriander seeds
juice of 1 lemon
1 tsp grated or ground nutmeg
2 bay leaves
2 tbsp oil
700g/1½lb rump steak
Saté Sauce (see page xx)
6 tbsp peanut butter
1 tbsp brown sugar
2 chilli (chili) peppers, seeded
1 tsp sugar
juice and rind of 1 lemon
⅔ cup/150ml/¼pt beef stock
1⅓ cup/225g/8oz long-grain rice, cooked

To prepare

♦ Place all the ingredients except the meat in a blender to make a paste.

♦ Trim the meat and cut into small squares. Mix with the paste and allow to marinate for several hours.

♦ Arrange the meat on skewers.

♦ Make the sauce by mixing all the ingredients except the lemon juice together in a saucepan. Bring to the boil and simmer for about 20 minutes. Add the lemon juice.

♦ While the sauce is cooking turn the grill (broiler) onto a high heat and allow the skewered meat to cook. Turn every 2 minutes for the first 6 minutes, then lower the heat and continue cooking. The time will depend on whether you like your meat slightly rare or well cooked.

To serve

Accompany with boiled rice (see page 10).

Serves 4

MADRAS BEEF CURRY

Curries are best made in advance as the spicy flavour improves with reheating.

Ingredients
6 tbsp vegetable oil
2 large onions, peeled
4 stalks celery, washed
700g/1½lb chuck steak (stewing meat)
1 tbsp flour
½ tsp paprika
½ tsp garam masala
1–2 tbsp Madras curry powder
1 bay leaf
1 tsp tomato purée (tomato paste)
2½ cups/600ml/1pt beef stock or water
1½ cups/425g/15oz canned peeled tomatoes
1 medium potato, peeled
Garnish
onion rings
1 tbsp chopped parsley
oven temperature 180°C/350°F/Gas 4

To prepare

♦ Heat 4 tablespoons oil in a large frying pan. Cut off a few thin onion rings for garnish, and then finely chop the remainder and cook for 5 minutes.

♦ Remove the strings from the celery and chop finely. Add to the onions and stir well for a further 2 minutes. Remove to a casserole or thick-bottomed saucepan.

♦ Trim the steak and remove any gristle. Cut into 2.5-cm/1-in cubes. Sprinkle with flour, seasoned with the paprika and garam masala. Add remaining oil to the frying pan and fry the meat until golden on all sides. Remove with a slotted spoon to the casserole.

♦ Sprinkle the curry powder and any remaining flour into the pan and simmer for 2 minutes. Add the tomato purée to the stock and pour into the pan, stirring well to remove meat juices. Add the canned tomatoes and bring to the boil.

♦ Meanwhile cut the potato into cubes and bring to the boil for 5 minutes in salted water.

♦ Add the tomato and curry mixture to the meat and onions. Stir well.

♦ Drain the potato cubes and add to the casserole with ½ teaspoon salt. Cook in the oven for 1 hour or until the meat is tender. Taste and season accordingly.

To serve

Serve with pilau or pilaf rice (see page 20), mango chutney and poppadoms or any of the other side dishes or sambals which are so popular with curry (see page 62).

Variation

This curry can be cooked on top of the cooker but remember to check from time to time that it is not sticking or drying out. Add a little stock or water if necessary.

MEXICAN CHILLI (CHILI)

Ingredients

2 onions, peeled
3 stalks celery, washed
2 tbsp vegetable oil
2 cloves garlic, crushed
2 cups/450g/1lb lean minced (ground) beef
1½ cups/425g/15oz canned peeled tomatoes
1 carrot, scraped
1–2 tsp chilli (chili) powder
1 fresh chilli pepper (chili), seeded
1 green pepper, seeded
1¾ cups/425-g/15-oz can kidney beans
1 bouquet garni
1¼ cups/300ml/½pt stock
1 cup/225g/8oz long-grain rice

To prepare

♦ Chop the onions finely and remove strings from the celery before chopping into thin slices.

♦ Heat the oil in a frying pan and cook the onions, celery and garlic over a low heat for 5 minutes.

♦ In a thick-bottomed saucepan heat 1 tablespoon oil over a medium heat and brown the minced beef, stirring to keep the meat in small pieces.

♦ When the meat is evenly browned add the cooked onion mixture and the whole can of tomatoes, including juice.

♦ Grate the carrot and add to the meat mixture. Add the chilli powder, finely chopped chilli pepper and diced green pepper. Finally add the kidney beans and bouquet garni. Mix well with stock and allow to simmer gently for 40 minutes.

♦ Cook the rice by the absorption method (see page 10).

Serves 4

BEEF KOFTAS

Ingredients

1 medium onion, peeled and finely chopped
1 clove garlic, crushed
2 cups/450g/1lb lean minced (ground) beef
2.5cm/1in piece fresh root ginger, grated
salt and freshly ground pepper
½ tsp coriander, crushed or ground
1 tsp fresh breadcrumbs
1 tbsp yoghurt
1 tsp freshly chopped parsley
½ tsp lemon juice
1–1¼ cups/225–275g/8–10oz rice
½ tsp turmeric
2 tbsp oil
2 tbsp chopped pineapple
1½ tbsp/25g/1oz flaked almonds

To prepare

♦ Sweat the onion and garlic in a little oil for about 4 minutes.

♦ Mix the minced beef in a bowl with ginger, seasoning, coriander, breadcrumbs, yoghurt, parsley and lemon juice.

♦ Add the onion mixture and mix thoroughly. Form into 8 sausage shapes.

♦ Meanwhile put the long-grain rice on to cook with the turmeric and 1 teaspoon of salt for 15 minutes when all water should have been absorbed.

♦ Place the minced beef mixture on wooden skewers. Brush with oil and brown under a hot grill (broiler), turning every 2 minutes to cook and brown evenly.

To serve

Mix the rice with the pineapple and serve in a heated dish scattered with flaked almonds. Serve the koftas on top. Serve cucumber and pineapple yoghurt as a side dish or Barbecue or Curry Sauce (see page 38).

Serves 4

Beef koftas

BEEF STROGANOFF

Ingredients
350g/¾lb fillet or rump steak
2 tbsp/25g/1oz butter
2 tbsp vegetable oil
1 small onion, peeled and finely chopped
3 spring onions (scallions), washed
1 tbsp flour
¼ tsp paprika
salt and freshly ground pepper
4 cups/225g/8oz mushrooms, washed and sliced
1 tbsp brandy
2 tbsp madeira or sherry
⅔ cup/125ml/¼pt beef stock
4 tbsp sour cream
Garnish
1 tbsp chopped parsley
¼ tsp paprika
1–1¼ cups/225–275g/8–10oz long-grain rice

To prepare

♦ Trim the steak and cut into thin strips about 5cm/2in long.

♦ Heat the butter and oil in a frying pan and cook the onion for about 4 minutes over a low heat until translucent. Add the chopped spring onions, retaining a few rings of green for final garnish.

♦ Meanwhile mix the flour with the paprika and seasoning and coat the meat strips evenly.

♦ Add the sliced mushrooms to the onions and sauté gently for another 2 minutes. Remove the onions and mushrooms with a slotted spoon, leaving as much fat behind as possible.

♦ Put the rice on to cook by the absorption method (see page 38). Heat serving dishes and plates.

♦ Over a fairly high heat fry the meat for a few minutes; less for fillet steak than for rump. Heat the brandy in a ladle and ignite it with a match.

♦ Pour over the steak and allow to flame. Remove the meat and mix with the onion and mushrooms.

♦ Add the madeira or sherry and any excess flour and paprika left over to the pan and stir well. Gradually add the stock, scraping all meat juices from the bottom of the pan. Add the meat, mushrooms and onions to the sauce and reheat for about 2–3 minutes. Turn the heat low. Add 2–3 tablespoons sour cream and mix well.

To serve

Serve in a ring of rice garnished with parsley, sour cream, onion rings and a sprinkling of paprika. A crisp green salad or crisply cooked green vegetable, such as mange toute (snow peas) or french beans, makes an excellent accompaniment to this luxurious but quickly prepared dish.

Serves 4

MARINATED LAMB CHOPS WITH SAVOURY RICE

Ingredients
8 best end of neck chops
Marinade
2 tbsp oil
2 tbsp soya sauce
1 tsp brown sugar
salt and freshly ground pepper
1 tsp lemon juice
Sauce
1 onion, peeled
2 tbsp sherry
2 tbsp water
2 tbsp redcurrant jelly
¼ tbsp ground coriander
1 cup/100g/4oz canned pineapple pieces
1 tbsp parsley
1⅓ cup/225g/8oz savoury rice (see page 17)
oven temperature 200°C/400°F/Gas 6

To prepare

♦ Place the chops in a plastic bag with the mixed marinade. Allow to soak for several hours. Turn the bag around on a dish to help the meat to contact the marinade.

♦ Arrange the chops on a rack over a roasting pan and place in a pre-heated oven. Cook for 15–20 minutes.

♦ Make the sauce by adding 1 tablespoon oil to a saucepan and cooking the finely chopped onion for 3 minutes. Add the remainder of the marinade from the chops and simmer for a few minutes. Add the sherry, water, redcurrant jelly, coriander, seasoning and pineapple pieces. Simmer for 15 minutes. The sauce may be blended before serving. Alternatively mix 1 teaspoon cornflour (cornstarch) with 1 tablespoon water, add a little warmed sauce and return to the saucepan. Stir until sauce is slightly thickened.

To serve

Lay the chops on a bed of savoury rice, sprinkled with chopped parsley. Pour sauce as you like.

Serves 4

LAMBS' KIDNEYS IN RED WINE

Ingredients
12 lambs' kidneys, skinned
1 tbsp flour
salt and freshly ground pepper
4 tbsp/50g/2oz butter
1 onion, peeled and sliced
3 cups/175g/6oz mushrooms, washed and sliced
2 tomatoes, skinned and chopped
⅔ cup/150ml/¼pt red wine
Garnish
1 tbsp parsley
1 cup/225g/8oz long-grain rice
oven temperature 180°C/350°F/Gas 4

To prepare

♦ Remove the core from the kidneys and cut in half. Dredge with seasoned flour.

♦ Heat the butter and gently cook the onion on a low heat. Remove from the pan into an ovenproof dish.

♦ Sauté the kidneys for a few minutes on either side until golden brown. Add mushrooms and continue cooking for about 2 minutes.

♦ Add the red wine and tomatoes. Spoon into the ovenproof dish, cover with foil and cook in the oven for 25 minutes.

♦ Cook the rice (see page 10).

To serve

Serve individual portions in a ring of rice on the plate and garnish with chopped parsley.

Serves 4

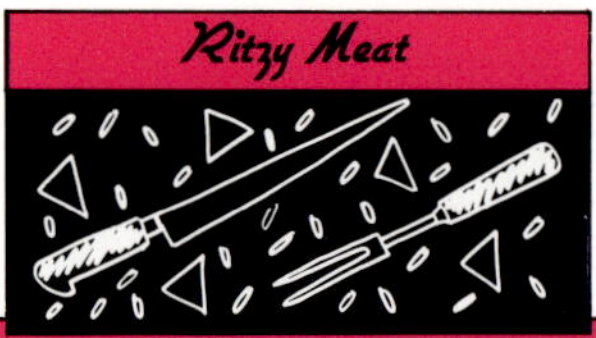

LAMB TIKKA WITH PILAU RICE AND CHILLI (CHILI) SAUCE

Ingredients

600g/1¼lb leg of lamb (cut in a thick slice)
⅔ cup/150ml/¼pt natural yoghurt
1 tsp chilli (chili) powder
1 tsp crushed coriander
1 tsp garam masala
½ tsp salt
juice of 1 fresh lime or lemon
1⅓ cups/225g/8oz pilau rice (see page 20)

Garnish

8 lettuce leaves
2 tomatoes, sliced
12 slices of cucumber
1 small onion, peeled and finely sliced
1 lemon or lime, quartered

To prepare

♦ Leg of lamb sliced about 1.2cm/½in thick is best for this dish. Remove any bone or gristle. Cut into 1.2-cm/½-in thick cubes.

♦ Mix yoghurt with all other ingredients in a plastic bag or a flat dish. Add the meat to the marinade and allow to soak for several hours. Turn from time to time.

♦ Divide the meat onto 4 skewers and cook under a hot grill (broiler), turning every two minutes.

To serve

Serve each portion off the skewer with pilau rice and a green salad. Garnish with the above ingredients and, if you like, add some Chilli Sauce (see page 38).

Serves 4

SOUVLAKIA (LAMB KEBABS) WITH RICE

This dish is delicious when cooked on a barbecue.

Ingredients
450g/1lb leg of lamb
12 bay leaves
juice of ½ a lemon
2 tbsp olive oil
salt and freshly ground pepper
1 tsp oregano
1⅓–1⅔ cups/225–275g/8–10oz long-grain rice, cooked

To prepare

♦ Allow one skewer for each person. Cut the lamb into small 2.5-cm/1-in cubes and thread onto the skewers with pieces of bay leaf in between. Leave space at either end of the skewers to enable them to rest on the grill (rack).

♦ Beat the lemon juice into the olive oil, season with salt, pepper and oregano and leave the lamb to marinate in the mixture in a plastic bag for at least 1 hour.

♦ Cook under a hot grill (broiler) for about 10 minutes turning occasionally, so that the lamb becomes well seared on the outside and tender and juicy inside.

To serve

Serve immediately with a tomato and cucumber salad, quarters of lemon to squeeze over the meat and a dish of cooked rice. Serve lemon juice or seasoned yoghurt on all types of accompanying salads.

Serves 4

LAMBS' LIVER WITH CREAM SAUCE

Ingredients
450g/1lb lamb's or calf's liver
2 tbsp seasoned flour
2 tbsp/25g/1oz butter
2–3 tbsp vegetable oil
1 large onion, sliced
1 clove garlic, crushed (optional)
2–3 tbsp medium sherry
⅔ cup/150ml/¼pt stock
¾ cup/200g/7oz canned peeled tomatoes, sliced
salt and freshly ground black pepper
3 tbsp whipping cream
1⅓–1⅔ cups/225–275g/8–10oz boiled rice
Garnish
1 tbsp freshly chopped parsley
oven temperature 180°C/350°F/Gas 4

To prepare

♦ Slice the liver into even sized pieces. Dip each piece into the seasoned flour until it is evenly coated.

♦ Heat the butter and oil in a frying pan on a low heat. Cook the sliced onion for 4 minutes until transparent and then transfer to a casserole. Sprinkle the remaining seasoned flour into the casserole and stir around.

♦ Carefully fry each slice of liver in the remaining fat for 1 minute on each side.

♦ Transfer the liver into the casserole. Add the sherry, stock and tomatoes to the frying pan and bring to the boil. Pour over the liver and cook for about 30 minutes.

To serve

Serve on a heated dish with a border of boiled rice (see page 10), sprinkled with chopped parsley.

Serves 4

SPICY LAMB RISSOLES

This is an excellent dish for using up left-over lamb from a joint (roast). These rissoles are also well suited to being made in advance and frozen until needed.

Ingredients

1 cup/225g/8oz minced (ground) lamb
2 tbsp vegetable oil
1 large onion, peeled and minced or finely chopped
½ tsp oregano
1 clove garlic, crushed
1 tbsp lemon juice
1⅓/225g/8oz cooked long-grain rice
2 eggs, beaten
salt and freshly ground pepper
¼ tsp ground cumin
½ tsp paprika
1 tbsp chopped parsley
1 tbsp flour
1½ cups/100g/4oz dried breadcrumbs
oil for frying
1¼ cup/300ml/½pt Spicy Tomato Sauce (see page 39)

To prepare

♦ Heat the oil in a large frying pan and cook the finely chopped or minced onion for 4 minutes. Push to one side of the pan and fry the lamb, separating the meat with a fork or a spoon.

♦ Mix the oregano, garlic, lemon juice and cooked rice and allow to cool in a mixing bowl.

♦ Mix together the eggs with 2 tablespoons water.

♦ Add the seasoning, cumin, paprika and parsley to the lamb mixture and mix well. Add a little beaten egg to bind the mixture together.

♦ With floured hands form rice and lamb mixture into 5-cm/2-in rissole shapes. Dip into the remaining egg and then into the breadcrumbs. Arrange on a tray and chill for at least 15 minutes before frying.

♦ Heat the oil in a deep fat pan and fry for 4–5 minutes.

To serve

Serve hot with a spicy sauce and a crisp green salad.

Serves 4

CROWN ROAST OF LAMB WITH APRICOT RICE STUFFING

This is an excellent dinner party dish as it can be prepared in advance.

Ingredients
2 best ends of neck (lamb)
1 tbsp oil
freshly ground pepper
Stuffing
½ cup/100g/4oz long-grain or risotto rice (see page 11)
1 tbsp butter
1 onion, peeled and finely chopped
2 stalks of celery
¾ cup/100g/4oz dried apricots, steeped or 1 large can apricots
1 tbsp sultanas (white raisins)
1 tbsp chopped mixed nuts
1 egg, beaten
1 tbsp chopped parsley
salt and freshly ground pepper
oven temperature 180°C/350°F/Gas 4

To prepare

♦ Ask the butcher to prepare the crown roast or, if this is not possible, have the best ends chined. Remove the skin from the fatty side of the joints. Cut along the fat about 3.5cm/1½in from the top of the bone and remove fat and meat from the tops of the bones. Scrape the little end bones clean with a knife. Turn the meat over the cut between the cutlets to enable the joint (roast) to bend.

Stand the two pieces of meat up with the bones at the top. Turn fatty sides in and sew together at the top and bottom of the joins to make the crown roast. Paint over with oil and sprinkle with pepper.

♦ For the stuffing, partially cook the rice for 10 minutes (see page 10), rinse and allow to drain and cool.

♦ Heat the butter and oil and cook the onion for 4 minutes over a low heat. Add the chopped celery, chopped apricots (if using canned apricots retain 8 drained halves for garnish), sultanas and nuts. Lastly stir in the rice. Turn into a bowl and allow to cool. Mix with the egg yolk and parsley.

♦ Fill the centre of the roast with the stuffing. Cover with a piece of foil.

♦ Cover the individual tips of the bones with foil to prevent charring. Then completely cover with foil. Roast in the oven for 1½–2 hours, depending on size of the cutlets.

♦ Any excess stuffing may be used to stuff apricot halves which can be cooked brushed with oil for the last 30 minutes of cooking time.

♦ Remove the crown roast to a heated plate and make gravy to accompany roast in the usual way. If using canned apricots, a little juice may be added to the gravy. Remove the string before carving through the cutlets.

PORK FILLET EN CROUTE

Ingredients
3 medium-size or 2 large pork fillets (tenderloins)
2 tbsp oil
Stuffing
½ cup/100g/4oz risotto rice (see page 11)
1 small onion, peeled
1¼ cups/300ml/½pt stock or water
1 small apple, peeled and diced
1 tbsp sultanas (white raisins)
1 tbsp mixed nuts
rind and juice of 1 lemon
1 tsp dried sage or 1 tbsp chopped fresh sage
salt and freshly ground pepper
1 egg, beaten
Pastry
250g/½lb frozen puff pastry
Gravy
1 tbsp flour
2–3 tbsp white wine
⅔ cup/150ml/¼pt stock
oven temperature 200°C/400°F/Gas 6 and 210°C/425°F/Gas 7

To prepare

♦ Trim the fat and gristle from the fillets. Cut into 15-cm /6-in lengths.

♦ For stuffing, heat the oil in a frying pan and cook the onion for 2 minutes. Add the rice and stir well for a further 2 minutes. Pour in the stock or water with ¼ teaspoon salt. Cover and cook for 5 minutes. Remove the lid and fork through the rice, then add the diced apple, sultanas, nuts, lemon rind and juice. Mix through with a fork, cover and continue cooking for 5 minutes. When all the stock has been absorbed the rice should be slightly undercooked. Put the mixture into a bowl and allow to cool. Mix in most of the egg, leaving a little for glazing the pastry.

♦ Place 2–3 lengths of fillets, slightly flattened, on a board. Cover with rice stuffing. Top with the remaining lengths of fillets and tie neatly into a round shape with string.

♦ Brush over with oil and wrap loosely in foil. Cook in a moderately hot oven for 35 minutes. Allow to cool and retain any meat juices for use in sauce.

♦ Roll the thawed pastry into an even shape, about 25cm/10in square. Place the cooled meat, with string removed, in the centre. Fold the pastry over the meat and damp the edges with cold water. Turn the pastry parcel over so that the fold is underneath. Fold the ends neatly, cutting a square out and placing flaps over like a parcel. Place on a baking sheet.

♦ Roll out any scraps of pastry and cut out leaves. Alternatively cut out decorative shapes with a cocktail (cookie) cutter. Wet the shapes and arrange them on the croute. Make sure there are several slits to allow steam to escape.

♦ Brush over with the egg. Cook in the oven at the higher temperature for 25 minutes then turn down and cook for a further 10 minutes.

♦ For a gravy scrape the meat juices into a saucepan. Add the flour, seasoning, white wine and stock. Whisk well and serve in a heated sauceboat when thickened.

Serves 4–6

SAUSAGES AND BACON ROLLS WITH TOMATO RICE

Ingredients
1 cup/225g/8oz long-grain rice
2½ cups/600ml/1pt beef stock
2 tsp tomato purée (tomato paste)
1 small onion, peeled and chopped
½ tsp salt
8 sausages
8 rashers (strips) bacon
1¼ cups/300ml/½pt Spicy Tomato Sauce (see page 39)
oven temperature 180°C/350°F/Gas 4

To prepare

♦ Wash the long-grain rice several times and drain.

♦ Mix the beef stock, tomato purée and onion with the salt and bring to the boil. Pour over the rice and fork through to stop grains sticking together. Cover and simmer until all liquid is absorbed, about 15 minutes.

♦ Turn the grill (broiler) on high and brown the sausages on each side for 3 minutes. Allow to cool slightly and then wrap bacon rashers around the sausages.

♦ Grill for a further 5 minutes under a medium heat. Alternatively cook in the oven in the tomato sauce for 15 minutes after browning under the grill (broiler).

♦ Arrange sausage and bacon rolls on the tomato rice and pour the sauce on top.

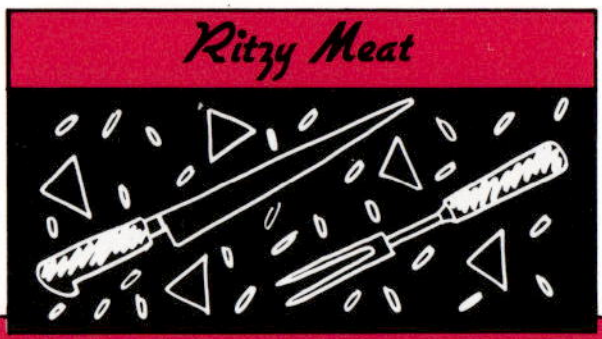

SWEET AND SOUR PORK WITH BOILED RICE

Ingredients
450-g/1-lb leg of pork, cut in a thick slice
1 small onion, peeled and sliced
2.5cm/1in fresh root ginger, finely chopped
1 clove garlic
1 tbsp dry sherry
2 tbsp soya sauce
salt and freshly ground pepper
Sauce
1 small red pepper, seeded
1 small green pepper, seeded
2 spring onions (scallions), washed
1¼ cups/150ml/½pt chicken stock
1 tbsp white wine vinegar
2 tsp brown sugar
1 tbsp tomato purée (tomato paste)
2 tsp cornflour (cornstarch)
Batter
3 tbsp cornflour (cornstarch)
2 tsp water
1 egg
oil for frying
1⅓–1⅔ cups/225–275g/8–10oz boiled rice
frying temperature 170°C/360°F

To prepare

♦ Cut the pork into 2.5cm/1in cubes after trimming away any fat or gristle.

♦ Mix up the marinade of onion, ginger, garlic, sherry, soya sauce and seasoning and allow the pork to stand in this for at least 1 hour, turning from time to time.

♦ Cut the peppers into 1cm/¼in cubes and chop the spring onions into thick rings.

♦ Place all other ingredients, apart from the cornflour, into a saucepan with the peppers and spring onions. Mix the cornflour with 2 tablespoons of cold water and then mix into the saucepan. Fry the meat before heating the sauce.

♦ Make up the batter in a deep plate, mixing the cornflour, water and egg together until thick.

♦ Drop the drained marinated meat into the batter. Make sure the fat is very hot before dropping the meat in, either with tongs or a slotted spoon. Cook for about 2–4 minutes until golden. Drain on kitchen paper.

♦ Heat the sweet and sour sauce and, when thickened and hot, add the fried pork.

To serve

Accompany with plain boiled rice (see page 11).

Serves 4

PORK FILLETS IN BRANDY CREAM SAUCE

Ingredients

700g/1½lb pork fillet (tenderloin)
1 tbsp flour
salt and freshly ground pepper
2 tbsp/25g/1oz butter
2 tbsp oil
1 onion, peeled and finely chopped
1⅓ cups/250g/8oz Herbed Rice (see page 16)
2 tbsp brandy
¼ tsp nutmeg
⅔ cup/150ml/¼pt single cream (cereal cream)

Garnish

1 lemon
1 bunch of watercress

To prepare

♦ Trim the pork fillets. Remove any gristle and excess fat. Cut into diagonal slices. Beat out to about 1cm/½in thick.

♦ Mix the flour with seasoning and coat each slice evenly.

♦ Heat the butter and oil in a frying pan and cook the onions for 4 minutes. Remove onto a plate with a slotted spoon.

♦ Prepare and cook the Herbed Rice.

♦ On a medium heat sauté the pork fillet slices for about 4 minutes each side until golden brown. Heat the brandy in a ladle and set alight. Pour onto the pork and allow to flambé.

♦ Serve the Herbed Rice on a warmed serving dish. Arrange the pork slices on top and keep warm in a low oven.

♦ Add nutmeg and single cream to the frying pan and stir over a low heat to combine the meat juices and cream. Pour the sauce over the meat.

To serve

Accompany with a crisp green salad. Garnish with 4 lemon wedges and watercress.

Serves 4

Sweet and sour pork with boiled rice

PORK SPARE RIBS IN BARBECUE SAUCE

Ingredients

Marinade

2kg/4½lb spare ribs
2 tbsp soya saucea
2 tbsp sherry
3 tbsp red wine vinegar
1 clove garlic, crushed
1 small onion, peeled and sliced
salt and freshly ground pepper
1 small piece root ginger, grated

Sauce

2 cloves garlic, finely chopped
3 spring onions (scallions), washed and chopped
½ tsp fennel seeds
½ tsp cinnamon
½ tsp basil
2 cloves
2 tsp brown sugar
juice of ½ lemon
juice of ½ orange
2 tbsp red wine vinegar
1¼ cup/300ml/½pt stock
2 tbsp soya sauce
1¾ cups/425g/15oz canned peeled tomatoes
⅔ cup/150ml/¼pt chicken stock

To prepare

♦ If possible ask the butcher to trim the spare ribs to a good handling size, about 10cm/4in long.

♦ Using a clean screw-top jar, place all the marinade ingredients together and mix well by shaking. Pour the marinade over the pork and turn from time to time for about ½–1 hour, or even longer, if you wish.

♦ Deep fry the spare ribs for about 5 minutes and drain on kitchen paper (kitchen towels).

♦ Mix the ingredients for the sauce in a saucepan, wok or frying pan and bring to the boil.

♦ Add the spare ribs and simmer in the sauce for about 30 minutes. Add a little water and the remaining marinade to the pan to prevent it going dry.

Serves 4

Variation

Cook the marinated ribs on a wire rack over a roasting pan in a hot oven at 210°C/425°F/Gas 7. Pour the sauce over the roasted meat.

SAVOURY SAUSAGE AND BACON KEBABS WITH TOMATO SAUCE

Ingredients
16 cocktail sausages (eg 'Vienna' sausages)
8 slices of bacon
8 mushrooms
1 green pepper, seeded
1 red pepper, seeded
4 bay leaves
4 tomatoes
2 tbsp vegetable oil
salt and freshly ground pepper
1¼ cups/300ml/½pt Spicy Tomato Sauce (see page 58)
1 cup/250g/8oz long-grain rice

To prepare

♦ Take 4 large or 8 small skewers to prepare the kebabs. If cocktail sausages are not easily available simply twist the longer chipolata-type (pork) sausage into two.

♦ Roll the bacon after flattening the slice with a knife. Each slice will make 2 small rolls.

♦ Remove the mushroom stems and cut the peppers into squares.

♦ Thread sausages, bacon, mushrooms, peppers and bay leaves alternately onto the skewers. Lay in a flat dish and pour the oil over. Season well. Turn in the oil for 10 minutes until well coated.

♦ Prepare the Tomato Sauce and the rice.

♦ Put the kebabs on when the rice has started to cook. Place them under a high grill (broiler) and turn the skewers round every 2 minutes until the food is evenly browned on each side. When it is golden brown turn the heat to medium and cook for 3–4 minutes each side. Lay the tomatoes on the grill for the last few minutes of cooking. Tomatoes are best cooked separately as they tend to fall off skewers when cooked.

To serve

Lay the kebabs on a bed of rice and serve with Tomato Sauce. If you wish to remove the skewers use a fork to slide the food off.

Serves 4

OSSO BUCO MILANESE

Ingredients
2 tbsp vegetable oil
4 tbsp/50g/2oz butter
1 onion, peeled and sliced
1 clove garlic, crushed
1 kg/2lb shin of veal with bone
⅔ cup/150ml/¼pt white wine
1¼ cup/300ml/½pt chicken or veal stock
3–4 cups/500g/1lb tomatoes or 1½ cups/425g/15oz canned peeled tomatoes
1 lemon, rind and juice
1–2 tbsp parsley
1⅓–1⅔ cups/225–275g/8–10oz Risotto Milanese (see page 18)
oven temperature 180°C/350°F/Gas 4

To prepare

♦ Heat the oil and butter in a heavy saucepan. Add the onion and garlic and cook for 3–4 minutes on a fairly low heat without browning. Remove onto a plate.

♦ Brown the veal on all sides on a medium heat.

♦ Add white wine and stock. Allow to cook for a few minutes. Either add the onion to the saucepan, standing the veal upright to prevent the marrow coming out of the bone, or transfer all ingredients into an ovenproof casserole in the same way.

♦ Add chopped tomatoes and simmer on top of the cooker (stove) or in the oven for about 1 hour or until the meat is tender. Add a few drops of lemon juice to the veal.

To serve

Mix the grated rind of a lemon with the chopped parsley and sprinkle over the Osso Buco. Serve with Risotto Milanese.

Serves 4

VEAL AND MUSHROOM CASSEROLE

Veal and mushroom casserole

Ingredients
700g/1½lb stewing veal
3 tbsp flour
salt and freshly ground pepper
100g/¼lb belly of pork
3 tbsp oil
4 tbsp/50g/2oz butter
2 onions, peeled and finely chopped
3 stalks celery, washed
2 carrots, scraped
1½ cups/425g/15oz canned peeled tomatoes
½ tsp oregano
¼ tsp nutmeg
1¼ cups/300ml/½pt beef stock
4 tbsp white wine
2 cups/100g/4oz mushrooms, washed and sliced
5 tbsp sour cream
Garnish
1 tbsp chopped parsley
1⅓–1⅔ cups/225–275g/8–10oz long-grain yellow rice (see page 13)
oven temperature 180°C/350°F/Gas 4

To prepare

♦ Trim and chop the veal into 2.5-cm/1-in cubes. Toss in seasoned flour. Cut the belly of pork into cubes.

♦ Heat the oil and butter in a frying pan and add the onions. Cook over a low heat for 3 minutes.

♦ Remove the strings from the celery and cut into small slices. Add to the onions. Dice or ring the carrots and add to the pan with the onions.

♦ Remove the vegetables with a slotted spoon after about 6 minutes to an ovenproof casserole.

♦ On a high heat fry the veal and belly of pork to seal for a few minutes, turning over from time to time until golden brown. Then add to the vegetables in the casserole. Add the remaining flour to the frying pan and pour the stock in. Whisk briskly to combine flour and meat juices.

♦ Add canned tomatoes, oregano, nutmeg and white wine. Pour over the meat in the casserole. Cover and cook for 1 hour.

♦ Add mushrooms and cook for a further 15 mins.

♦ Stir in sour cream at the last minute and garnish with parsley. Serve with yellow rice.

Ritzy Birds

BOKARI PILAF

Ingredients
450g/1lb chicken livers
4 tbsp vegetable oil
2 onions, peeled and diced
1 clove garlic, crushed
2 carrots, scraped and grated
1½ cups/350g/12oz basmati or long-grain rice
salt and freshly ground pepper
½ tsp turmeric
2½ cups/600ml/1pt chicken stock
¾ cup/200g/7oz canned tomatoes or 3 tomatoes, skinned
2 tbsp parsley, chopped

To prepare

♦ Trim and dice chicken livers.

♦ Heat the oil in a large pan and fry the livers until golden brown.

♦ Add the onions, garlic and carrots to the chicken livers and turn with a spoon for about 2 minutes.

♦ Add the washed rice, seasoning, turmeric and stock. Cover and cook for 20 minutes. Remove the lid and stir gently. Add the chopped tomatoes and cook for a further 5–10 minutes until the rice is tender.

♦ Sprinkle with chopped parsley and turn into a heated serving dish.

Serves 4

CHICKEN AND WILD RICE SALAD

Ingredients

¾ cup/175g/6oz long-grain and wild rice, cooked

1⅓ cups/225g/8oz cooked chicken, chopped

1 small onion, peeled

⅔ cup/150ml/¼pt well-flavoured mayonnaise (see page 32)

1¾ cup/100g/4oz mushrooms, washed

1 tbsp lemon juice

4 tbsp sweetcorn (corn kernels)

7 black olives

salt and freshly ground pepper

1 lettuce

2 heads chicory

To prepare

♦ Cook the rice as directed on the packet of mixed long grain and wild rice (2 cups/450g/16oz water – 1 cup/225g/8oz rice, see page 11). Allow to cool.

♦ Add the chopped chicken to the cooled rice.

♦ Chop the onion finely and add to the mixture with the mayonnaise.

♦ Slice the mushrooms thinly. Mix with the rice, remembering to retain a few for the top of the salad. Pour the lemon juice over the retained mushrooms.

♦ Add the sweetcorn and 4 chopped olives to the mixture. Season to taste.

♦ Arrange the lettuce and sliced chicory in the salad bowl. Turn the chicken and rice mixture into the bowl.

To serve

Garnish with the mushroom slices and the 3 remaining black olives.

Serves 4

FRIED CHICKEN WITH ALMOND RICE AND HOLLANDAISE SAUCE

Ingredients
4 chicken portions, boned
½ cup/50g/2oz plain (all purpose) flour
1 tsp paprika
6 tbsp oil
1 onion, peeled and finely chopped
1 cup/225g/8oz long-grain rice
2 spring onions (scallions), washed and chopped
2½ cups/600ml/1pt chicken stock
½ tsp turmeric
⅓ cup/50g/2oz slivered almonds
Hollandaise Sauce
¾ cup/175g/6oz butter
2 tsp butter
6 peppercorns, slightly crushed
1 tbsp wine vinegar
2 egg yolks
1–2 tsp lemon juice
salt and freshly ground pepper

To prepare

♦ Dip the chicken portions in a mixture of flour and paprika. Pat the coating well into the chicken and chill for 10 minutes.

♦ Heat 2 tablespoons oil in a large saucepan and gently cook the onion over a low heat.

♦ Add the rice and stir well. Sprinkle on the spring onions. When the rice is well coated with oil gradually pour in the hot chicken stock and turmeric. Cover and cook until all the stock has been absorbed.

♦ Heat the remaining oil over a fairly high heat, and brown the slivered almonds. Remove and drain.

♦ Fry the chicken until golden on each side, about 3 minutes to seal on each side. Reduce to medium heat and continue until cooked through. This will take a further 8 minutes.

♦ To make the hollandaise sauce use a double boiler or an ovenproof bowl over a saucepan of water (make sure the water is not touching the bottom of the bowl). Cut the butter into pieces and place in the bowl over a low heat to melt. Place the water, peppercorns and wine vinegar in a small saucepan and allow to reduce to about 1 tablespoon. Whisk the egg yolks with the reduced liquid and about 1 tablespoon melted butter. The mixture should become thick and creamy. Continue adding the melted butter in a thin stream, whisking or stirring briskly all the time. As the mixture becomes thick and creamy add a few drops of lemon juice at a time. Taste for flavour and season accordingly.

♦ Stir the browned almonds into the cooked rice.

To serve

Lay the fried chicken portions on the rice and accompany with the hollandaise sauce. Serve a crisp green vegetable, such as French beans, broccoli or mange tout (snow peas).

Serves 4

CHICKEN SATÉ

Ingredients

Marinade

1 spring onion (scallion), washed and chopped

2.5cm/1in fresh root ginger, grated

grated rind of 1 lemon

¼ tsp ground cinnamon

6 cardamom pods

1 tsp cumin

1 tsp ground coriander

1 tsp peanut butter

⅔ cup/150ml/¼pt Coconut Milk (see page 62)

approx 4 cups/700g/1½lb chicken without bone

Sauce

6 tbsp peanut butter

1 onion, peeled and finely chopped

2 fresh chilli (chili) peppers, seeded

1 clove garlic, crushed

juice of 1 lemon

2 tbsp chicken stock or 2 tbsp Coconut Milk

Garnish

1 spring onion (scallion), chopped

To prepare

♦ Make up the marinade by mixing all the ingredients with the coconut milk.

♦ Cut the chicken into small pieces.

♦ Marinate the chicken overnight in the refrigerator or at least for several hours. Remove from the marinade and thread onto wooden or metal skewers.

♦ Mix all sauce ingredients together and cook for 10 minutes. (The best sauce is made by blending all ingredients together.)

♦ Grill (broil) the chicken skewers for 4 minutes each side under a high heat. Then allow to cook for a further 4 minutes each side under a medium heat. This dish is also delicious cooked on the barbecue.

To serve

Serve with boiled rice or a rice salad. Garnish sauce with chopped spring onion.

Serves 4

CHICKEN BROCHETTES WITH ORANGE SAUCE

Ingredients

700g/1½lb chicken breasts

rind and juice of 2 oranges

1 tbsp oil

salt and freshly ground pepper

Sauce

4 tbsp redcurrant jelly

2 tbsp/25g/1oz butter

4 tbsp red wine

2 cloves

¼ tsp ground nutmeg

juice of 2 oranges

4 tbsp water

1 tsp cornflour (cornstarch)

Green rice ring

1⅓ cups/225g/8oz cooked long-grain rice

3 tbsp chopped parsley

1 spring onion (scallion), finely chopped

salt and freshly ground pepper

3 tbsp salad oil

1 tbsp white wine vinegar

Garnish

orange slices

oven temperature 180°C/350°F/Gas 4

To prepare

♦ Skin and trim the chicken breasts. Remove bone if it is still attached. Cut into 2.5-cm/1-in pieces.

♦ Mix half the orange rind with all the orange juice, oil and seasoning and pour over the chicken pieces. Allow to stand in the refrigerator for at least 1 hour. Turn over from time to time to allow juice to penetrate.

♦ Thread the chicken pieces onto skewers.

♦ To make the sauce place all the ingredients except the water and cornflour in a saucepan with the remainder of the marinade. Allow to simmer gently for 10 minutes.

♦ To make the rice ring mix the cooked rice with the parsley, spring onion and seasoning. Mix the salad oil and vinegar separately and pour over the rice. Pack into a well oiled ring mould. Heat in the oven for 15 minutes.

♦ Brush the chicken brochettes with oil and cook under the grill (broiler), turning from time to time for about 10 minutes: 2 minutes under a high heat each side and the remaining time under a medium heat.

♦ Finish the sauce by blending the cornflour with the water. Add some heated sauce to the cornflour mixture and return to the saucepan. Stir until the mixture thickens slightly.

♦ Turn out the rice ring on to a heated serving plate and place the brochettes on top.

To serve

Garnish with slices of orange. Serve sauce separately.

Serves 4

FRIED CHICKEN WITH SPICED RICE AND ALMONDS

Ingredients
2 cups/350g/¾lb chicken breasts
1 tbsp flour
½ tsp paprika
4 tbsp/50g/2oz butter
⅓ cup/50g/2oz slivered almonds
1 onion, peeled and finely chopped
2 tbsp vegetable oil
1 cup/225g/8oz basmati rice
chicken stock
1.5cm/½in fresh root ginger, grated
1 tbsp soya sauce

To prepare

♦ Cut the chicken breasts into strips about 0.5cm/⅓in.

♦ Mix the flour and paprika and coat each strip of chicken.

♦ Heat the butter over a medium heat and fry the almonds until golden on each sides. Remove to a plate with a spoon.

♦ Lower the heat and cook the onion until translucent for 3–4 minutes. Remove from the pan.

♦ Add the oil and, on a fairly high heat, cook the chicken strips for 5 minutes turning until golden on all sides. Remove from the pan.

♦ Wash the basmati rice thoroughly in about 5 changes of water. Drain well before adding to the frying pan. Gradually add the chicken stock, stirring with a fork. Cover and cook for 15 minutes.

♦ Remove the lid and stir in the onions, chicken and ginger. Gradually add the soya sauce and cook for 5 mins.

To serve

Sprinkle the dish with almonds and a little extra paprika. Decorate with a few petals of almonds.

Serves 4

ROAST CHICKEN WITH RICE AND MUSHROOM TIMBALES

Ingredients
1 roasting chicken, approximately 1.5kg/3½lb
½ lemon
1 bay leaf
¼ onion, peeled
sprig of thyme or 1 tsp mixed herbs
2 tbsp/25g/1oz butter
Rice Timbales
2 cups/100g/4oz mushrooms, washed and sliced
4 tbsp/50g/2oz butter
2 tbsp lemon juice
1⅓ cups/225g/8oz long-grain rice, cooked
salt and freshly ground pepper
1 tbsp parsley, chopped
1 tbsp grated cheese
1 small carrot (optional)
Gravy
1 small onion
1 bay leaf
1¼ cups/300ml/½pt chicken stock
1 tbsp flour
2 tbsp white wine (optional)
oven temperature 200°C/400°F/Gas 6

To prepare

♦ Rub over the chicken with the halved lemon. Place the lemon, bay leaf, onion and herbs inside the cavity of the chicken with a small knob of butter.

♦ Rub the remaining butter over the chicken skin and place in a pre-heated oven. Cook for approximately 1 hour 20 minutes or until chicken is tender.

♦ Slice the mushrooms. Heat the butter in a frying pan and sauté the mushrooms for 3 minutes. Add the lemon juice. Cover the pan and allow all moisture to evaporate without burning the mushrooms.

♦ Have the rice already cooked by the absorption method (see page 9). Mix with salt and pepper, parsley and grated cheese.

♦ Oil small moulds or ramekin dishes well. Arrange mushroom slices on the bottom. If you wish, slice some carrot with a cocktail cutter for extra decoration. Blanch the slices in boiling water for 4 minutes, then add to the mushroom design. Mix remaining sliced mushrooms with the rice. Turn the rice into the moulds and pack down well.

♦ Place the moulds in the oven for the last 20 minutes of the chicken's cooking time.

♦ Remove the chicken and moulds from the oven and allow to stand for 10 minutes before carving and turning out the timbales.

♦ To make gravy remove the chicken from the roasting pan and keep warm. Pour off excess fat. If giblets come with the chicken simmer these for at least 30 minutes with an onion, bay leaf and water for stock. Otherwise use bought chicken stock. Add the flour to the chicken juice in the roasting pan which can be placed over a low heat. Whisk the flour and chicken juices together. Add seasoning and, for extra special gravy, white wine. Gradually add the stock and stir until smooth and slightly thickened. Serve in a heated sauce boat.

♦ Carve the chicken and serve 1–2 rice timbales with each portion.

Serves 4

PAELLA

Ingredients

6 tbsp oil

2 large onions, peeled and finely chopped

2–3 cloves garlic, crushed

1¼ cups/275g/10oz long-grain rice

salt and freshly ground pepper

¼ tsp turmeric

2½ cups/600ml/1pt chicken stock

1 red pepper, seeded

1 green pepper, seeded

1 cup/225g/8oz white fish, boned

⅔ cup/150ml/¼pt white wine

1 bay leaf

4–8 chicken drumsticks

4 cups/450g/1lb mussels

¾ cup/100g/4oz peeled prawns

Garnish

1 tbsp chopped parsley

To prepare

♦ Heat the oil in a large frying pan or casserole. Over a low heat cook the onions until they become translucent. Add the garlic.

♦ Gradually add the rice and stir around in the onions and oil until the grains are coated with oil.

♦ Add seasoning and turmeric to the hot stock and pour on to the rice gradually, stirring as the rice is brought to the boil. Cover with a lid or with foil, and simmer gently for 10 minutes.

♦ Meanwhile dice the green and red peppers and blanch for 1 minute in water.

♦ Poach the white fish in water with a little of the wine and the bay leaf for about 5 minutes.

♦ Fry the drumsticks in another pan in 2 tablespoons oil until golden brown and cooked.

♦ Clean the mussels by removing the beards and rinsing several times in cold water. Any which remain open when tapped should be discarded. Pour the wine into a saucepan with a little fish stock from the poached fish. Add the mussels and shake the pan from time to time until the mussels open. This will take about 8 minutes. Keep warm.

♦ Remove the lid from the rice and separate the grains with a fork. Add the peppers stirring gently, the white fish, prawns, about ⅔ cup/150ml/¼pt mussel stock and then the chicken. Cover and cook until rice is separate and liquid is absorbed. Add chopped parsley and decorate with parsley before serving.

ORIENTAL DUCK

Ingredients

1 duck, approximately 2kg/4lb
4 spring onions (scallions), washed

Marinade

3 tbsp soya sauce
2 tbsp honey
1.2cm/½in fresh root ginger, grated
rind and juice of 1 lemon
2 tbsp sherry
2 tbsp vegetable oil

Accompaniment

4 tbsp stock or water
3 cups/200g/7oz water chestnuts
3 cups/225g/8oz bean shoots
1 tbsp sherry and soya sauce (optional)
1⅓ cups/225g/8oz boiled rice (see page 9)

Gravy (optional)

1 small onion
salt and freshly ground pepper
1 tbsp flour

oven temperature 200°C/400°F/Gas 6
reducing to 180°C/350°F/Gas 4

To prepare

♦ Remove the giblets from the duck. Place the duck in a dish or plastic bag.

♦ Chop the spring onions and place half in a small bowl with the ingredients of the marinade. Mix well and pour over the duck. Allow to stand in the refrigerator. If you are using a plastic bag turn the duck from time to time. Otherwise baste the duck with the marinade. Allow the duck to marinate for several hours or overnight for the best flavour.

♦ Remove the duck from the marinade. Place it on a rack on top of a roasting pan. Put in the oven at the higher temperature for 30 minutes to crisp.

♦ Turn down the heat and cook for a further 1¼ hours.

♦ Tip the remaining marinade into a saucepan and bring to the boil. Add the stock or water and simmer for 5 minutes. Then add the sliced water chestnuts, bean shoots, the remaining spring onions, and, if you wish, the sherry and soya sauce. The vegetables should be timed to be served with the cooked duck.

♦ The duck giblets may be boiled with water, onion and seasoning to make gravy.

♦ In order to do this remove the duck from the oven and cut any string away. Keep the duck warm on a serving plate. Pour off the excess fat into a heatproof dish, leaving the duck juices behind. Add the flour to the juices. Stir over a heated ring and season well. Add ⅔ cup/150ml/¼pt giblet stock and whisk until a rich gravy is made.

To serve

Pour over the carved duck, and accompany with vegetables and boiled rice.

Serves 4

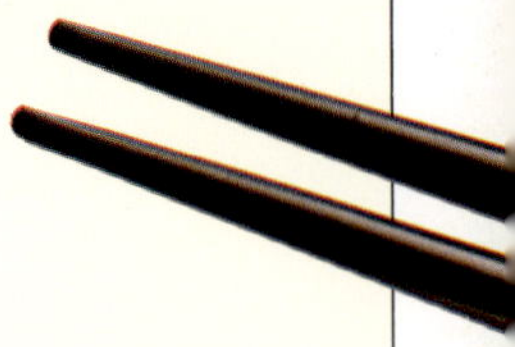

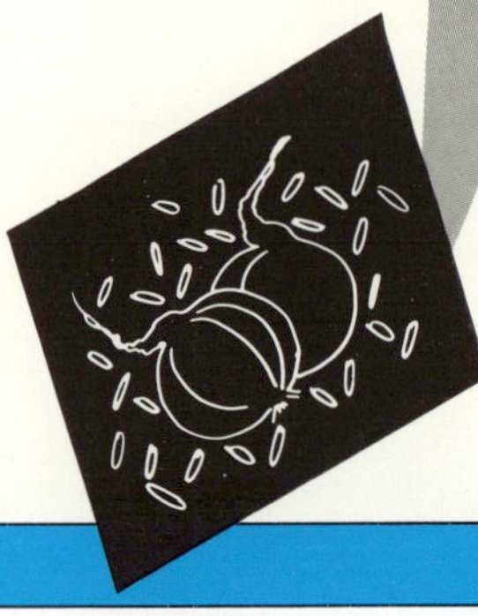

CHICKEN BIRIANI

Ingredients
1 cup/225g/8oz long-grain rice, preferably basmati
1 tbsp salt
2 large onions, peeled
2 cloves garlic, crushed
2.5cm/1in piece root ginger, grated
6 tbsp vegetable oil
2–3 boned chicken portions
1 tbsp flour
¼ tsp chilli (chili) powder
1 tsp cumin, ground
5 tbsp yoghurt
1 tbsp lemon juice
4 tbsp water
1 tsp ground coriander
¼ tsp ground cinnamon
½ tsp turmeric
⅓ cup/50g/2oz slivered almonds
Garnish
onion rings
1 hard-boiled (hard-cooked) egg
1 tomato, skinned
oven temperature 150°C/300°F/Gas 2

To prepare

♦ Wash the rice several times. Allow to soak in a large bowl of water and salt for at least 1 hour.

♦ Slice half an onion finely into rings and reserve. Place the remaining onion, garlic, ginger, 1 tablespoon oil and some water in an electric grinder or food processor with a few slivered almonds. Grind to a paste.

♦ Heat the remaining oil on a fairly high heat and fry the onion rings until golden brown. Remove with a slotted spoon and drain on kitchen paper (kitchen towels).

♦ Fry the remaining slivered almonds until golden on each side and drain with the onion rings.

♦ Cut the chicken into small pieces and toss in seasoned flour mixed with the chilli powder. Fry until golden and drain onto paper.

♦ Fry the paste in fat. Add the yoghurt, 1 tablespoon at a time, with lemon juice. Add 4 tablespoons water and return the chicken to cook over a low heat for 15 minutes.

♦ Add the coriander, cumin and cinnamon to the chicken after 5 minutes and stir well.

♦ Meanwhile cook the rice in 4½ cups/1l/1¾pt boiling salted water with the turmeric for 10 minutes and drain.

♦ Spread the drained rice on top of the chicken casserole. Add the almonds.

♦ Cover the mixture with foil and then the casserole lid, and bake in the oven for 35 minutes.

To serve

Mix the chicken and rice well with a fork and turn into a heated serving dish. Garnish with sliced hard-boiled eggs, and browned onion rings. Serve with such accompaniments as Cucumber Raita (see page 63), mango chutney, poppadoms, chapatis or a Vegetable Curry (see page 48).

Serves 4

TURKEY ESCALOPES WITH WHITE WINE AND MUSHROOM SAUCE

Ingredients
2 large turkey breasts, boned
1 tbsp flour
¼ tsp paprika
2 tbsp/25g/1oz butter
2 tbsp vegetable oil
1 medium-sized onion, peeled
2 cups/100g/4oz mushrooms, washed and sliced
2–3 tbsp white wine
Sauce
1¼ cups/300ml/½pt milk
1 slice of onion
1 bouquet garni
1 bay leaf
4 slightly crushed peppercorns
1½ tbsp/20g/¾oz butter
3 tbsp/20g/¾oz flour
salt and pepper
1⅓ cup/225g/8oz savoury rice (see page 17)

To prepare

♦ Cut the turkey breasts in half and place the halves between a sheet of foil or cling film (plastic wrap) and beat out to an escalope shape with a rolling pin.

♦ Mix the flour with the paprika and coat the turkey.

♦ Heat the butter and oil in a frying pan and over medium to high heat fry on both sides until golden. They will need about 5 minutes each side. Keep warm in a low oven.

♦ Cut one thick slice from the onion and cut the remainder into fine dice. Over a low heat cook the onion in the pan with oil from the turkey. After 3 minutes add the mushrooms and stir occasionally. Add the white wine and leave for 2 minutes over a very low heat.

♦ Meanwhile put the milk with the slice of onion, bouquet garni, bay leaf and peppercorns on a low heat. Allow to come to almost boiling point. Then turn the heat off. Leave to infuse for 10 minutes covered.

♦ Melt the butter in a small saucepan, add the flour and make a roux. Stir for 1 minute, then strain in the infused milk gradually to make a béchamel sauce. Cook until smooth. Add the onion and mushroom mixture and cook for a further 2–3 minutes.

To serve

Serve with savoury or plain boiled rice. Place the escalopes on the rice and pour the mushroom sauce over the escalopes and rice.

Variation

This dish can also be made with veal escalopes.

Serves 4

Ritzy Seafood

Jambalaya

SALMON COULIBIAC

Ingredients
450g/1lb fresh salmon
2 tbsp white wine
1 bay leaf
1 bouquet garni
⅔ cup/150ml/¼pt water
freshly ground pepper
½ onion
Filling
4 tbsp/50g/2oz butter
1 onion, peeled and finely chopped
1¾ cups/100g/4oz mushrooms, washed
1⅓ cup/225g/8oz cooked long-grain rice
1 tbsp chopped parsley
¼ tsp chopped dill
salt and freshly ground pepper
2 hard-boiled (hard-cooked) eggs, shelled and chopped
Pastry
450g/1lb frozen puff pastry, thawed
1 egg
oven temperature 210°C/425°F/Gas 7

To prepare

♦ Place the salmon in a deep saucepan, preferably on a trivet. If this is not available, place the fish on a piece of double foil, with two ends reaching up the sides of the saucepan, as this will make it easy to remove from the pan.

♦ Place the white wine, bay leaf, bouquet garni, water, pepper and ½ onion in a saucepan and bring to the boil, simmer for 10 minutes.

♦ Pour the liquid over the salmon and bring to the boil again. Turn the heat low as the salmon must be allowed to poach very gently for 15 minutes. Allow less time if the fish is in steaks. The liquid should only move slightly in the saucepan. Allow to cool in the fish liquor.

♦ Remove the fish from the saucepan and take off the skin. Remove any bones, and flake.

♦ For the filling heat the butter in a frying pan and cook the onion over a low heat for 4 minutes. Push to one side of the pan.

♦ Slice the mushrooms and add to the pan. Allow to cook for 3 minutes. Add the rice, herbs and seasoning. Mix well. Allow to cool.

♦ Divide the pastry into 4 pieces. Roll out one piece of pastry on a work surface into a 20cm/8in square.

♦ Divide the rice mixture into 4 portions and the salmon into 4 equal servings. Put half the first rice portion in the centre of the rolled-out pastry and place 1 salmon portion on top. Finally cover the other half of the first rice portion. Damp the edges of the pastry with cold water and fold the corners to the centre. Pinch the edges together, enclosing the filling. Repeat for the other 3 pastry parcels.

♦ Flake and flute the edges of the pastry and decorate with pastry leaves. Allow to rest in the refrigerator for 20 minutes. Glaze with beaten egg and cook in a pre-heated oven for 30 minutes until golden brown.

To serve

Accompany with Hollandaise Sauce (see page 58).

KEDGEREE

This makes an excellent breakfast dish for guests as it can be prepared in advance and heated through just before serving.

Ingredients
½ cup/100g/4oz long-grain rice
3 hard-boiled (hard-cooked) eggs, shelled
salt and freshly ground pepper
1 cup/225g/8oz smoked haddock
⅔ cup/150ml/¼pt milk
1 bay leaf
1 slice of peeled onion
Garnish
1 tbsp chopped parsley
½ tsp paprika
1 lemon, quartered

To prepare

- Cook the rice by the absorption method (see page 9).
- Chop 2 hard-boiled eggs. Sieve the white and yolk of the third egg separately to garnish the top of the kedgeree.
- Add the 2 chopped eggs to the rice, with the salt and pepper.
- Place the smoked haddock in a saucepan with the milk, bay leaf, onion and a little pepper. Bring to the boil and allow to simmer for 5 minutes. Allow to cool slightly in the milk. Remove and flake the fish from the skin. Add to the rice.
- Heat all the ingredients together and pile onto a heated serving dish.

To serve

Garnish with rows of egg yolk, egg white and chopped parsley with a little paprika. Serve with lemon quarters.

Serves 4

JAMBALAYA

Ingredients
2 tbsp/25g/1oz butter
2 tbsp oil
1 onion, peeled and finely chopped
4 stalks celery
1 green pepper, seeded
2 aubergines (eggplant)
1 cup/225g/8oz long-grain rice
2½ cups/600ml/1pt chicken stock
1 tsp salt
freshly ground black pepper
1 tbsp Worcestershire sauce
1 tsp soya sauce
⅔ cup/100g/4oz cooked, diced ham
1½ cups/225g/8oz peeled prawns (shrimp)
3 tbsp chopped parsley
oven temperature 180°C/350°F/Gas 4

To prepare

♦ Heat the butter and oil in a frying pan and cook the onion over a low heat until translucent.

♦ Wash the celery and peel the strings from the rounded side with a sharp knife. Cut into small pieces. Add to the onions.

♦ Dice the pepper and aubergines. Add to the celery and onion and stir for a few minutes to mix well. Add the rice and stir if there is room in the pan. If there is not, put the vegetables and rice into a large casserole and mix well.

♦ Mix the stock with the salt and pepper, Worcestershire and soya sauce.

♦ Transfer the vegetables and rice into the casserole if not already there. Add the stock over a medium heat. When the liquid comes to the boil cover with a lid and cook in the oven for 20 minutes.

♦ Remove from the oven. Stir in the prawns and ham. Replace the lid and cook for a further 10–15 minutes until the rice is cooked. Taste for seasoning.

♦ Mix with chopped parsley before serving.

To serve

This dish can be garnished with whole prawns.

Serves 4

NASI GORENG

Ingredients
6 cups/450g/1lb long-grain rice
salt
2 tbsp oil
2 medium onions, peeled
2 cloves garlic, crushed
2 fresh chilli peppers (chilis), seeded
1 tsp garam masala
4 tbsp oil
2 tbsp soya sauce
½ tsp Worcestershire sauce
¾ cup/100g/4oz cooked prawns (shrimp)
250g/8oz cooked chicken
1⅓ cups/100g/4oz cooked ham
3 eggs (or 4 if making the omelette) (omelet)
salt and freshly ground pepper

Garnish
1 tbsp chopped spring onions (scallions)

To prepare

♦ Cook the long-grain rice in 5 cups/1200ml/2pt boiling water with 1 teaspoon salt (see page 9). Fork through the grains to make sure they are separated before putting on the lid.

♦ Heat 2 tablespoons of oil in a frying pan. Add 1 finely chopped onion and the garlic, and cook until translucent. Remove with a slotted spoon.

♦ In a blender or food processor whizz together the other chopped onion and chilli peppers, the garam malasa, and the soya and Worcestershire sauces to make a paste.

♦ Add the remaining oil and fry the paste over a medium heat for about 3 minutes.

♦ Add the prawns, chicken and ham and stir for a few minutes. Beat the eggs with salt and pepper. Turn the heat up fairly high and add the egg mixture, stirring continuously until the egg begins to set.

♦ Add the cooked rice and blend with the other ingredients on a lower heat.

Serves 4

Variation

If you like Nasi Goreng garnished with omelette (omelet) strips, use 4 eggs. Add 2 to the meat and prawn mixture and make a small omelette with the other two.

For an omelette, take 2 eggs. Mix vigorously with a fork. Add seasoning. Melt a knob of butter in an omelette pan over a high heat. Pour in the egg mixture and pull the cooked edges back from the sides of the pan to the centre (do not mix as if you were making scrambled egg). When mixture is almost set place the pan under a hot grill (broiler) for about 1 minute. Turn onto a board and cut into thin strips.

To serve

Decorate the top of the rice dish with the omelette strips. Add a few chopped spring onions (scallions) for garnish.

Nasi goreng

ORIENTAL CRABMEAT SALAD

This dish should be served as a starter (appetizer).

Ingredients

- scant 1 cup/200g/7oz-can crabmeat or meat from 1 cooked crab
- 1⅓ cups/225g/8oz cooked long-grain rice
- 1 red pepper, seeded
- 1 green pepper, seeded
- 1 cm/¼in fresh root ginger, grated
- 1½ cups/100-g/4-oz can bean sprouts
- 2 tbsp soya sauce
- ⅔ cup/150ml/¼pt Vinaigrette Dressing (see page 30)

To prepare

♦ Remove the meat from the crab, including the claws, with a skewer, and place it in a bowl. Mix with the cooked rice.

♦ Cut the peppers into thin strips. Blanch in boiling water for 2 minutes. Drain in a sieve and cool by running under the cold tap.

♦ Add to the crab meat and rice.

♦ Mix the grated ginger with the bean sprouts and soya sauce over a low heat for 4 minutes. Allow to cool.

♦ Mix with the Vinaigrette Dressing

Serves 4

Variation

This mixture can be served hot without the French Dressing. Fry 1 small, finely chopped onion in 4 tbsp/50g/2oz butter for 4 minutes. Add the peppers and ginger and cook for a further 4 minutes over a low heat. Then gradually add the other ingredients. Stir until heated through.

PAMPLONA RICE

Ingredients
6 tbsp vegetable oil
1 large onion, peeled and finely sliced
2 chilli peppers (chilis), seeded
1 red pepper, seeded
1 green or yellow pepper, seeded
1½ cups/350g/12oz cod, boned and skinned
1¾ cups/425g/15oz canned peeled tomatoes
1¼ cups/275g/10oz long-grain rice
3 cups/750ml/1¼pt water
salt and freshly ground pepper
½ tsp turmeric or a few drops of yellow colouring

Garnish
1 tomato, sliced
1 lemon, quartered
oven temperature 180°C/350°F/Gas 4

To prepare

♦ Heat the oil in a large pan. Cook the onion for 4 minutes over a low heat.

♦ Slice the peppers into strips. Add to the onion with the choped chilli peppers, and cook for a further 2 minutes. Push to one side of the pan. Raise the heat a little and add the chunks of fish. Fry on each side. Season well.

♦ Add the tomatoes. Stir well. Add the rice. Stir round in the mixture.

♦ Add ¾ teaspoon of salt and turmeric or yellow colouring to the water. Gradually pour over the rice. Allow to cook for 10 minutes after the water has come to the boil. Turn the heat down and simmer gently.

♦ Turn into an ovenproof dish and allow to dry off in the oven. Fork through the mixture after 5 minutes.

Serves 4

Variation

1 can of anchovies can be used with 12 green olives to top this rice dish. Arrange and allow the dish to heat through again in the oven for 5 minutes. All tomato sauces (see pages 51 and 58) go well with this.

Oriental crabmeat salad

RICE STUFFED PEPPERS

Ingredients

4 red or green peppers
¾ cup/175g/6oz long-grain rice
a pinch of saffron powder or turmeric
2 tbsp/25g/1oz butter
1 onion, chopped
1 clove garlic, crushed
2 cups/100g/4oz mushrooms, thinly sliced and blanched
¾ cup/175g/6oz-can tuna fish, drained or
¾ cup/100g/4oz peeled prawns (shrimp), chopped
1 tbsp chopped parsley
salt and freshly ground pepper
1¼ cups/300ml/½pt Quick Tomato Sauce (see page 51)
oven temperature 180°C/350°F/Gas 4

To prepare

♦ Blanch the whole peppers in salted water. Drain. Cut off the tops and scoop out the seeds.

♦ Cook the rice with a pinch of saffron or turmeric in boiling salted water for 15 minutes until just cooked.

♦ Strain and rinse in cold water. Drain well.

♦ Melt the butter and soften the onion and garlic. Add the mushrooms, tuna, rice and parsley. Mix well and season to taste.

♦ Spoon into the peppers and place in a well-greased dish. Cover with buttered paper or foil. Surround with the tomato sauce and bake in a moderate oven for 30 minutes.

To serve

Sprinkle with any extra parsley.

Serves 4

Variation

Substitute the fish for 1⅓ cups/225g/8oz cooked chicken and 2 peeled, chopped tomatoes.

Rice stuffed peppers

PRAWN (SHRIMP) AND CUCUMBER SALAD

Ingredients

1⅓ cups/225g/8oz long-grain yellow rice, cooked (see page 13)

4 spring onions (scallions), washed

½ cucumber

1 generous cup/175g/6oz shelled prawns (shrimp), cooked

1 green pepper, seeded

salt and freshly ground pepper

juice of 1 lemon

⅔ cup/150ml/¼pt Vinaigrette Dressing (see page 30)

Garnish

whole prawns (shrimp) with shells, cooked

To prepare

♦ Tip the cooked, cooled rice into a bowl and fork through to separate the grains.

♦ Chop the spring onions finely and add to the rice.

♦ Cut half the cucumber into thin slices to surround the rice when served. Chop the remainder into cubes and add to the rice mixture with most of the prawns. Retain a few to decorate the top. Mix well.

♦ Cut the pepper into thin rings and keep a few for decoration. Add to the rice mixture. Mix well with salt, pepper and lemon juice. Then add the dressing.

To serve

Arrange on a plate surrounded by cucumber. Top with a few prawns and pepper rings which have been dipped in dressing. Garnish with whole prawns if you wish.

Serves 4

Ritzy Puddings

CREAMY RICE PUDDING

Ingredients

2 tbsp/25g/1oz butter

¼ cup/50g/2oz short-grain rice

1¼ cups/300ml/½pt evaporated milk

1¼ cups/300ml/½pt water

1 tbsp/25g/1oz sugar

½ tsp ground nutmeg

oven temperature 150°C/300°F/Gas 2

To prepare

♦ Butter an ovenproof pie dish (pie plate) well.

♦ Wash the rice several times in a sieve with running cold water. Drain.

♦ Pour the evaporated milk and water into the pie dish and sprinkle the rice on top. Add the sugar and stir well. If time allows leave to stand in the refrigerator for 1–2 hours as this improves the pudding.

♦ Sprinkle with nutmeg and add a few small pieces of butter to the surface.

♦ Bake in the oven for 30–40 minutes on a low shelf, then stir well to separate the grains. Continue cooking for a further 1–1¼ hours.

♦ This will produce a rice pudding with a skin on top which many people enjoy. If no skin is wanted cover with loose foil.

Serves 4

PINEAPPLE RICE PUDDING

Ingredients

1 Creamy Rice Pudding (see opposite)
2 tbsp soft brown sugar
4 slices canned pineapple, drained
4 glacé cherries

To prepare

♦ Make the Rice Pudding and cook covered in foil to prevent a skin forming.

♦ Remove the foil after 1¼ hours and sprinkle with the brown sugar and arrange the pineapple rings on top. Return to the oven for a further 30–40 minutes.

To serve

Decorate with glacé cherries in the centre of each pineapple ring.

Serves 4

Pineapple rice pudding

PINEAPPLE FRUIT FLAN

Ingredients
Short Crust Pastry
1½ cups/175g/6oz plain flour
a pinch of salt
4 tbsp/50g/2oz hard margarine or butter
2½ tbsp/35g/1¼oz white fat
1 egg, separated
2–3 tbsp water
Filling
1½ tbsp/25g/1oz ground rice
1¼ cups/300ml/½pt milk
2 tbsp/25g/1oz butter
grated rind of 1 lemon
juice of ½ lemon
1 tsp sugar
½ tsp cinnamon
1 egg yolk
2 egg whites
1 tbsp sherry
1¼ cups/150ml/10oz pineapple pieces
Garnish
6 pieces of pineapple
6 glacé cherries
oven temperatures 200°C/400°F/Gas 6 180°C/350°F/Gas 4

To prepare

♦ To make the pastry, sieve the flour into a bowl and cut the fat into small nut-sized pieces. Rub the fat in with the tips of the fingers until the mixture resembles fine breadcrumbs. Mix with egg yolk and add a little water, using a round-bladed knife until a smooth consistency is obtained. Tip onto a lightly-floured board and knead lightly until smooth. Place in a refrigerator for at least 15 minutes.

♦ Roll the pastry into a round about 3.5cm/1½in larger than the flan ring (pie plate). Lift the pastry on a rolling pin and ease gently into the ring without stretching. Roll the top with the rolling pin and prick the bottom. Bake and cover with a piece of greaseproof (waxed) paper weighted with baking beans for 15 minutes at 200°C/400°F/Gas 6.

♦ Meanwhile make up the sauce for the filling by whisking the ground rice, milk, butter, grated lemon rind, a few drops of juice, sugar and cinnamon over a low heat until thick. Allow to cool.

♦ When the mixture is fairly cool beat in the egg yolk and sherry.

♦ Chop or purée the fruit and line the bottom of the flan ring.

♦ Whisk the egg whites until fluffy but do not overbeat and fold into the rice mixture with a metal spoon. Tip into the flan ring and decorate with pieces of pineapple and cherries.

♦ Bake in the oven at the lower temperature for 25 minutes.

Serves 4

RICE MERINGUE

Ingredients
¼ cup/50g/2oz short-grain rice
1½ tsp/7g/¼oz butter
2½ cups/600ml/1pt milk
rind of 1 lemon
1 tbsp/25g/1oz sugar
2 eggs, separated
2 tbsp raspberry jam
½ cup/50g/4oz sugar
oven temperatures 150°C/300°F/Gas 2 180°C/350°F/Gas 4

To prepare

♦ Wash the rice several times in a sieve under the cold tap. Drain.

♦ Butter an ovenproof dish and sprinkle the rice into the dish. Cover with the milk, lemon rind and sugar. Stir well.

♦ Cook in the oven at the lower temperature for 30 minutes. Remove, add the egg yolks and stir well. Continue cooking for a further 1 hour covered with foil.

♦ Remove from the oven and spread the surface with jam. Allow to cool slightly.

♦ Whisk the egg whites until light and fluffy. Add half the sugar and continue whisking until the mixture is glossy. Fold in the remaining sugar keeping back ½ teaspoon to sprinkle on top.

♦ Pile the meringue mixture on top of the pudding and sprinkle with sugar. Return to the oven at the higher temperature and bake for 25 minutes when the topping will be golden and crisp on top.

Serves 4

Pineapple fruit flan

APRICOT RICE MOULD (MOLD)

Ingredients
½ cup/100g/4oz short-grain rice
½ cup/100g/4oz sugar
6 tbsp/75g/3oz butter
3¾ cups/900ml/1½pt milk
4 eggs, separated
1 vanilla pod or a few drops of vanilla essence (extract)
⅔ cup/150ml/¼pt whipping cream
2 tbsp/15g/½oz gelatine (gelatin)
2 cups/425g/15oz-can apricots

To prepare

♦ Wash the rice several times in a sieve and allow to drain.

♦ Add the sugar and butter to most of the milk in a saucepan. Retain ⅔ cup/150ml/¼pt milk to mix with the egg yolks. Heat the milk, vanilla pod, butter and sugar. If using vanilla essence add at the end of cooking.

♦ Sprinkle the rice into the milk mixture and stir over a low heat until the rice is cooked. Add a little of the hot rice mixture to the egg yolks and milk and return to the saucepan for the last 5 minutes of cooking time. Allow to cool.

♦ Whip the cream lightly.

♦ Make up the gelatine by sprinkling it into ⅔ cup/150ml/¼pt hot apricot juice in a heatproof cup. Stand the cup in boiling water and stir to completely dissolve the gelatine.

♦ Chop or blend half the apricot halves. Stir into the rice mixture with the gelatine. Allow to stand for 10 minutes.

♦ Whisk the egg whites until light and fluffy, but not to the cotton wool (hard peak) stage.

♦ Fold the cream and vanilla essence into the rice mixture and lastly fold in the egg whites. Turn into a large mould or cake pan and allow to set.

To serve

Decorate with the remaining apricots.

Serves 4–6

RICE SOUFFLE PUDDING

Ingredients
½ cup/100g/4oz short-grain rice
⅓ cup/75g/3oz sugar
4 tbsp/50g/2oz butter
3¾ cups/900ml/1½pt milk
4 eggs, separated
1 vanilla pod or a few drops of vanilla essence (extract)
Sauce
1¼ cups/300ml/½pt blended pineapple
2 tsp cornflour (cornstarch)
2 tbsp water
oven temperature 190°C/375°F/Gas 5

To prepare

♦ Rinse the rice well several times in cold water and allow to drain in the sieve.

♦ Sprinkle the rice into a pan of hot water. Bring to the boil and cook for 3 minutes. Drain and pour boiling water from the kettle over the grains.

♦ Add the sugar and half the butter to most of the milk, keeping some to mix with the egg yolks. Add the vanilla pod at this stage but if you are using vanilla essence add it at the end of the cooking. Heat the mixture and add the rice. Cook until tender for about 30 minutes. After 15 minutes add a little of the hot rice to the egg yolks and milk and then return to the rice. Stir well for the remainder of the cooking time. Allow to cool slightly.

♦ Butter a 17.5-cm/7-in soufflé dish. Pre-heat the oven. Put 1.2cm/½in water in the bottom of a roasting pan.

♦ Whip up the egg whites to a fluffy consistency but do not over-beat. Fold the vanilla essence and egg whites into the rice mixture and turn into a soufflé dish standing in the water. Cook for 25–30 minutes.

♦ For a sauce any blended fruit or fruit juice will do. Mix the cornflour with the water and add to the blended fruit. Heat over a low heat until slightly thickened.

To serve

This soufflé should be served straight from the oven.

Serves 4–6

IMPERIAL RICE MOULD (MOLD) WITH KIWI FRUIT

Ingredients

⅓ cup/75g/3oz short-grain rice
⅓ cup/75g/3oz sugar
½ cup/75g/3oz candied fruit
2½ cups/600ml/1pt milk
3 egg yolks
2 tbsp/14g/½oz gelatine (gelatin)
2 tbsp water
1¼ cups/300ml/½pt whipping cream
2 tsp Kirsch
a few drops of vanilla
3 tbsp/50g/2oz redcurrant jelly
2 kiwi fruit, peeled and sliced

To prepare

♦ Wash the rice and drain. Mix with the sugar and candied fruit in a saucepan. Pour in 2 cups/450ml/¾pt milk and allow to stand for at least 30 minutes.

♦ Mix the egg yolks with the remaining milk.

♦ Cook the rice in a saucepan, uncovered, by bringing the milk almost to the boil and then stirring over a low heat for about 15 minutes or until the rice is tender. Add the egg yolks and milk for the last few minutes of cooking. Allow to cool.

♦ Make up the gelatine by sprinkling it into 2 tablespoons of boiling water. It should dissolve but if the water has cooled too much stand the heatproof container in boiling water for a few minutes to make sure.

♦ Whip the cream lightly. Flavour with the Kirsch.

♦ Wet a mould. Place in the refrigerator to chill.

♦ Stir the gelatine into the cooled rice with the vanilla and lastly fold in the whipped cream. Pour into the mould and leave to set.

♦ Warm the redcurrant jelly. Unmould the rice onto a serving plate and run the slightly warmed jelly over the top.

To serve

Decorate with fruit.

Serves 6

MANGO AND KIWI HEDGEHOG

Ingredients
2 ripe mangoes
2 ripe kiwi fruits
approx 2 cups/425g/15oz canned creamy rice pudding or Creamy Rice Pudding (see page 116)

To prepare

♦ Cut the mangoes in half. Remove the stones. Run a small, sharp knife in straight lines down each half, scoring the fruit without cutting the skin.

♦ Turn the halved, marked fruit inside out carefully.

♦ Peel the kiwi fruits and slice. Arrange the kiwi slices in between the mango cubes.

♦ Divide the rice into 4 portions on serving plates and top with the mango hedgehogs.

Serves 4

RICE EGGS WITH PEACH SAUCE

Ingredients
⅓ cup/75g/3oz short-grain rice
¼ cup/50g/2oz sugar
3 egg yolks
1¼ cups/300ml/½pt milk
1/2 tsp vanilla essence (extract)
1 tbsp sultanas (white raisins)
1 tbsp mixed nuts, chopped
To coat
1 egg
1½ cups/125g/4oz dried breadcrumbs
To fry
4½ cups/1l/1¾pt vegetable oil
frying temperature 170°C/325°F/Gas 3
Peach Sauce
1 small can of peaches
2 tsp arrowroot

To prepare

♦ Wash the rice several times in cold water. Bring to the boil in a pan of water and boil for 10 minutes. Drain into a sieve.

♦ Cook the rice and milk in a saucepan until the rice is soft. Use a double boiler if you prefer. Otherwise stir over a low heat to prevent sticking.

♦ Add sugar and vanilla and stir until the mixture leaves the sides of the pan. Turn out onto a plate. Chill.

♦ Divide into pieces about the size of a small egg and roll on a floured board.

♦ Dip the croquettes in egg and breadcrumbs and deep fry in the vegetable oil until golden brown.

♦ To make the peach sauce, sieve or blend the fruit.

♦ Mix the arrowroot with a little cold water and stir into the fruit mixture.

♦ Heat over a low heat until thickened and serve with the croquettes.

To serve

Sprinkle with sultanas and mixed nuts and serve with cream, custard or a fruit purée sauce.

Serves 4

SHORTBREAD

Ingredients

1½ cups/175g/6oz plain (all-purpose) flour
½ cup/75g/3oz ground rice
1 cup/250g/8oz butter
½ cup/100g/4oz sugar
a pinch of salt
oven temperature 170°C/325°F/Gas 3

To prepare

♦ Sieve the flour and ground rice into a bowl.

♦ Making sure the butter is fairly soft, place it in another bowl and add the sugar. Squeeze the sugar and butter together by hand so they mix well but it is not necessary to cream the mixture.

♦ Add the salt to the flour and then gradually work in the lump of butter and sugar until a smooth ball is formed.

♦ Turn out onto a floured surface which is a mixture of ground rice and flour. Knead until smooth. Roll out 2 balls, shape in a thistle mould (decorated mold) and turn onto a baking sheet. If a shortbread mould is not available cook two cakes in 15-cm/6-in flan rings (pie plates) or sandwich pans. Mark the edges.

♦ Cook in the oven for 1 hour.

♦ Sprinkle with sugar when cooling.

Makes 2 cakes

Variation

This mixture may be rolled out and cut into biscuit shapes which will only take 20 minutes to cook.

Alternatively, to make a delicious fruit shortcake, roll the mixture into an oblong about 1.2cm/½in thick. Cut off one oblong 17.5cm/7in long × 7.5cm/3in wide. Use the one as a base and cut the other into triangles. Once the shortbread pieces have been cooked, spread thick cream on the base, cover with fruit and decorate with the wedge shapes. Any suitable fruit can be used.

INDEX

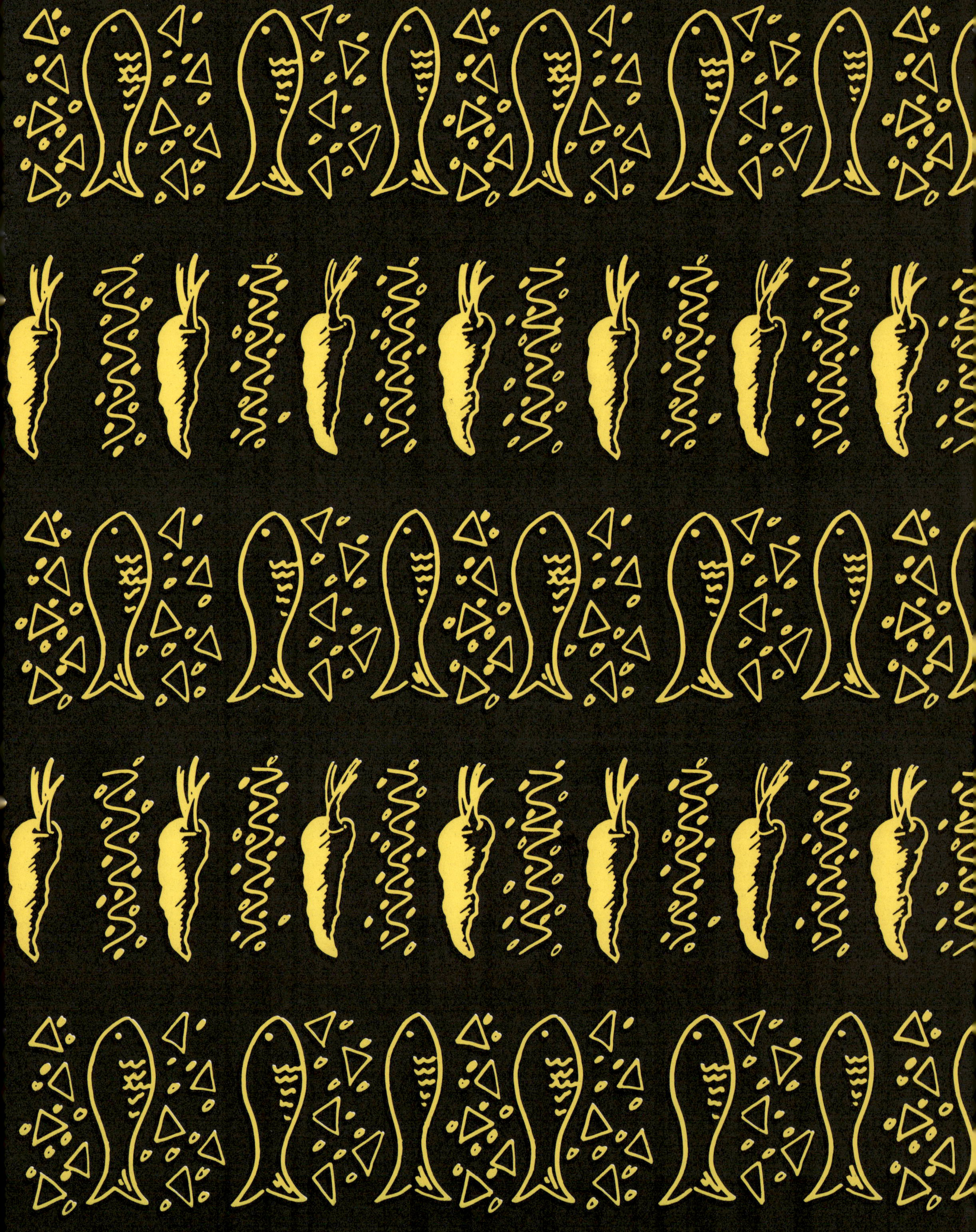